Praise for *Conversations i*

"*Dana takes you inside the beauty shop, and shows you that outside beauty is not the only thing happening there. The connections that are made can cause a beauty that goes far beyond our outside appearance. It's deep and funny at the same time. You'll love your time at the beauty shop! Fun read!*"

~ Mick Petersen International Best Selling Author

"*People place their secret lives in the hairdresser's hands. Dana shows you the beauty of the connections made inside the beauty shop. Love the lessons and truths of this story!*"

~ Monica DaMaren, International Best Selling Author, Coaching and training coordinator ProctorGallagher Institute

"*This book made us laugh out loud, but, also made us think bigger! We loved how Dana shows us that we all hear God's voice of truth! Loved the spirit of the beauty shop and the truths told inside. Great!*"

~ Willie and Tabitha Tart, International Best Selling Authors

Published by
Hasmark Publishing, judy@hasmarkservices.com

First Edition

Disclaimer

This book is designed to provide information and motivation to our readers. It is sold with the understanding that the publisher is not engaged to render any type of psychological, legal, or any other kind of professional advice. The content of each article is the sole expression and opinion of its author, and not necessarily that of the publisher. No warranties or guarantees are expressed or implied by the publisher's choice to include any of the content in this volume. Neither the publisher nor the individual author(s) shall be liable for any physical, psychological, emotional, financial, or commercial damages, including, but not limited to, special, incidental, consequential or other damages. Our views and rights are the same: You are responsible for your own choices, actions, and results.

Editor
Lex Maritta
lexmaritta@gmail.com

Cover Design
Eleanor Krueger

Book Design
Anne Karklins
annekarklins@gmail.com

ISBN-13: 978-1-988071-49-7
ISBN-10: 1988071496

Conversations in the Beauty Shop

Diana,
I'm so
grateful you
in my life! You
gold! Use your
key! ♥ D

A NOVEL

Dana Williams

*"Nothing damages the soul more than words,
but nothing lifts the soul more than words."*

*Pleasant words are a honeycomb sweet to the soul
and healing to the bones.
Proverbs 16:24*

*To My Husband and Sons:
You are my great adventure! Not to mention my greatest teachers.
Your love and laughter has made my life rich and beautiful.*

*To My Grandma:
You gave me your love for books and a good story.
Your love and truth is light to my soul.*

Acknowledgements

The Voice of Truth, for your imunmeasurable love, for creation and passion, for the written word. Thank you for your freedom and your light. My cup overflows with your abundance! You have my heart!

Mark Williams, My husband, and partner. You are my greatest fan! Your words of encouragement kept me moving when the voice of doubt would try to stop me. Thank you for always seeing me through eyes of love, and believing in my dreams. I am forever grateful for you!

Marcus Williams, thank you for sitting me down in front of the computer in November 2014 to listen to Peggy McColl talk about her program *The Millionaire Author*. That was the push I needed for this dream to become a reality. Your belief in me has helped me believe! Thank you for always challenging me to grow and being a voice of truth! I'm grateful!

Sam, you are always a voice of truth and I thank you for you help with this book. Reading it and critiquing it with love and care. Your perspective helped me to feel confident to tell the story. Your belief carried me! I'm grateful!

Dad, thank you for always wanting the best for me. Even though I can't see you anymore I feel you and know you're with me.

Mom, thank you for teaching me to be a strong woman, and for your adventurous spirit. As you always said, we have the gypsy blood. I feel your spirit with me!

Memaw, thank you for listening and letting me read to you! Your encouraging words lifted me when I doubted.

Donna my sister, you are truly the calm in my storms of life. Your belief and encouragement have carried me all of my life. Thank you for always answering the phone and talking me off the ledge!

The Sisterhood, my girlfriends, I can not list you all, but you know who you are. Your love and support has been a life preserver for me. You all have made up so much of my life story. Thank you for sharing my laughter and tears. You make me smile! You're gold!

Marci and Bob (Granny and Gramps as the boys call you.). There are not words to express my gratitude for all you have done to make this book a reality! Thank you for giving me a writing sanctuary, and so much more. I promise to pay it forward!

Peggy McColl, *New York Times* Best Selling Author and Best Seller maker, you're amazing! One of the best decisions I've made in my life was taking your course, *The Millionaire Author*. You are such a giver. The knowledge you have and the ability to teach it, is a gift. I'm grateful to have been a receiver of it. The moment I met you I felt a connection to you, as did my sons who now call you Auntie Peggy. Thank you for what you do! You inspire!

Eleanor Krueger, you nailed it! My book cover is exactly what I imagined. You listened to me and created my vision. You're amazing! I'm so grateful to have you in my life! Thank you for your belief in me and my story.

Judy O'Beirn and the Hasmark crew, you have not just loved and cared for my book, but, for me as well. Your expertise is such a comfort to the author. I get to have fun writing and you make it amazing! I cannot begin to share the gratitude in my heart for all you do! Thank you for an amazing experience.

Last but not least, The Beauty Shop (*my people*). This book is because of all of you, and for all of you. Everyone's story matters. I wanted to share the beauty inside the beauty shop. It's in all of you! The stories told to me in confidence I treasure and honor. I know all will be curious as to who maybe they are. I will tell you that all characters are no one person. You may find a piece of yourself in every one of them. I celebrate you all and thank you for the gift of serving you and discovering myself in all of you! My deepest gratitude to you!

Table of Contents

Dedication v
Acknowledgements 6
Foreword by Peggy McColl 9
Chapter 1. Big Girl Panties 11
Chapter 2. The Good, The Bad, And The Ugly 19
Chapter 3. My Angels 24
Chapter 4. The Silver Lining 32
Chapter 5. What School Doesn't Teach You 47
Chapter 6. Happy Pants 64
Chapter 7. Survival 68
Chapter 8. Changes 75
Chapter 9. More To Learn 83
Chapter 10. Closures 96
Chapter 11. Born For This 102
Chapter 12. More People "Lois" 107
Chapter 13. More People "Connie Sue" 108
Chapter 14. Pete 109
Chapter 15. It's All About Me (Lessons From A Narcissist) 111
Chapter 16. Life Keeps On Teaching And So Do People 113
Chapter 17. Stay Grateful 115
Chapter 18. Keep Loving(Five Years Later) 121
Chapter 19. Time Fliesys (5 Years Later) 123
Chapter 20. All's I'm Saying 126
About the Author 127
Sales Page 128

Foreword by Peggy McColl

Dana Williams has written an inspiring, thought-provoking book that encapsulates friendship, happiness and success. *Conversations in the Beauty Shop* is pure and understated, and yet so inspiring and deeply profound at the same time.

This book has the capacity to take you on a journey you may have never walked before that will lead you to a path of self-realization in a new way.

We follow Hannah's journey as she proves that you can find love and happiness in all areas of your life if you just listen to your heart, grow from your experiences, and let go of the past.

Throughout the book Hannah offers life-changing advice on self-discovery and personal development. She teaches that when a person starts accepting responsibility for the choices they make in their life, they unleash a power from within.

I feel honoured to be invited to write the foreword for this book. Dana has been a client of mine for years, and from the moment I met her, I knew she had a powerful message. Dana is a woman of action; she has great clarity on her purpose and has moved forward without hesitation to manifest the exact life she wants. By putting her knowledge into book form, she has empowered you to do the same.

> '*I would rather try and fail then never try at all. You see, I've learned the pain of regret is much greater then the pain of failure*'
>
> ~ Dana Williams, Excerpt from *Conversations in the Beauty Shop*

One of the things people are constantly searching for is happiness. Unfortunately, we tend to look in the wrong place and only choose things that make us happy for a short period of time. Too many people nowadays look externally for happiness but the only place enduring happiness can be found is within. This book does a great job reminding us of this important fact.

Happiness comes when we figure out how to acknowledge and accept the things we can't change, and how to take control of the things we have power over. It can just be realizing your strengths, what you are good at and enjoy, and how to be the person that you were truly meant to be. This isn't to say that there will not be obstacles along the way; it just means that those obstacles don't have to stop us from finding our place in the world and living our dreams.

One of the most important things you can do in this life is determine your attitude. Do you want to be happy or do you want to walk around every day feeling in the dumps? I personally choose to be happy and that is how I live my life.

This book provides the simplest purpose of life: to be happy and successful in all you do. This book will help you take action with your own life as it encourages you to use the power within yourself to change your life. It does a good job of tying together the seemingly diverse areas of human relationships, self-growth, and business ventures.

Dana brings a fresh perspective to improving our relationships with ourselves and everyone else in our lives. Everyone can relate to this book because there are so many different lessons to get out of Hannah's story. This book profoundly resonated with me and I can only hope it will resonate with you, too.

This book has given me a new perspective on my own life: where I've been, how I got there, and how to move forward. I encourage anyone who is tired of being unhappy or feeling stuck to read this book. We can courageously let go of what's holding us back, and begin living an abundant life filled with purpose, tranquility, and love.

Hannah says it best: "*We may not all be famous but we are all powerful! And we all have the power to fan the flame in one another.*"

Peggy McColl, *New York Times* Best-Selling Author
http://PeggyMcColl.com

CHAPTER 1

Big Girl Panties

The idea of spending time with strangers, and making them feel beautiful? Well it's scary. I'm 18 years old, fresh out of beauty school, and I have dreamed of this day forever. Now it's here… wow! I'm thinking back to how I made the decision to be a cosmetologist, it sounds important right? I originally thought I would be a Marine biologist, but dear ol'Dad, he set me straight. He said, "sister that's crazy, you need a safe career. Do you want a family?" Well yes Dad, I do want a family. "Well being out in the middle of the ocean with babies at home? You better think it over. I did, and here I am." There was also a family friend, Manny Hubbard, who shared with me that in the depression times, his Mother and Grandmother would always wear their same dress, but had a jar, and they would save up just to get their hair done. So he said to me, "no matter what, you will always have a job, because that is always going to be a priority for women." It helped to know that. I do love people and I have always loved messing with hair. It seems like the perfect job for me. I now have a job offer, but it requires me to move to a small mountain town, Tall Pines, New Mexico. So I've loaded up my Volkswagon Rabbit with all that I own, and hit the road for Tall Pines.

Two and a half hours later I'm driving into town, and oh it's beautiful here. It seems as though the mountains touch the sky, and the sky is a true blue. With the puffiest white clouds, it's like a movie set. This is one of those places you vacation in, and wish you could stay and live. Well I get to! I will stay with a cousin of my new boss. I met her once, and we hit it off, you know how you can sometimes meet a person and just feel at home? Well that's how I felt when I met Juanita. She's 10 years older than me, going through a divorce with a 5 yr old son. I will help her out with rent, and hopefully it will be a win-win situation.

As I pull up the driveway, Juanita and her son Jack are on the deck waving. I have a good feeling about my new life. I'm a big girl now, as my Dad would say. They come down to help me unload, and we make our way, with all that I own into the house. I love it, Juanita has a knack for decorating and has made me feel right at home. Jack is excited to show me my room, which is next to his. I am pleased with it. I especially love the light coming from the window, and the beauty I see looking out. I settle in and make my home, setting my few treasures out and making my room my own. You know how girls are, we like our nests to be filled with what makes us feel happy! As I'm making my bed, my thoughts wander and I try to envision my life in Tall Pines. Will I live here forever? Is my husband here? Will I be happy here? Will I be a good Cosmetologist ? What if I screw up someone's hair? Will I make enough money to live on? Oh, now panic sets in. I'm hearing many voices, all telling me I could fail. I sit down on my bed and I hear the voice of truth. It's my Grandma saying to me, "you're a child of God, and his plan is always for good, child do not fear!" Oh a calm comes over me, and my storm is over! Thank you Grandma, thank you God.

Jack is peeking in my door, he is such a cute little boy. I ask him to come in, and he wants to share a toy with me. I settle on the mustang matchbox car. Juanita calls for dinner and Jack goes running. Juanita is also a wonderful cook! I think to myself, she seems to be the perfect wife! I wonder what happened? We finish dinner and I clean up and do the dishes, while Juanita bathes and puts Jack to bed. My new family. Funny how life is not what you had pictured, but it's okay, and it's good. Goodnight, Juanita and Jack.

I feel really tired, and it's only nine. Juanita said the high altitude will make you feel tired, until you get used to it. I mean, I'm 18 and I normally would just be going out. I am missing my best friend Ruth. I'll call her tomorrow. I guess it's also all the change. As quick as I lay my head down, I'm asleep. I awake to Jack's voice. He is full of energy and very excited for the day. Juanita is patient with him. I ask her if there is anything I can do, and she starts to share how hard it is to be a single Mom! Even though Jack's Dad helps, he is two hours away, and it's hard to be there all the time for Jack. Also the visits with Dad make it hard on him. She feels the guilt of divorce. She just needs someone to hear her, and be the voice that tells her, *she will be okay, and so will Jack*. I sure don't have the life experience she has, but I do pay attention to others lives, and have listened to my elders, even though they don't think that I have. I also come from divorce, so I can give her the feelings of a child of divorce. So I share what I know, and tell her never to talk bad about his Dad in front of him, no matter her feelings. I now know God has a plan for me here, to encourage and remind them, they are loved and will be okay. The voice of truth. Me God?

I take a drive to try and get familiar with Tall Pines. The beauty here is *breathtaking*, as Grandma would say. I get to my new workplace to meet my new boss, Evan Cruz. He will give me my keys, and the rules of my new job. I'm feeling nervous, but try to keep my professional composure. Oh, the big girl panties are on and I think I have a wedgie! I now feel like I want my Mommy! Evan is a small man, but good-looking and is very full of himself, or do we say, has good self-esteem? He begins with how great he is, and how the women flock to him for their hair! So far it's the Evan show. As he shows me around the salon and explains how thing are done, he pats my butt! I want to say something, but I don't. He tells me, he will be training me to do things his way, so I will stay close to him most of the time. He wants me to feel like I'm young and dumb! I hate that! Why does anyone think it's ever ok to talk down to somebody? Oh, and the pat on the butt? What is that? I'm feeling a little nervous now, that I have made a wrong decision to work with Evan. But what would I do? I love it here, and I have committed to Juanita for my rent, and she is depending on it. Plus, I don't have money to just move again. So I will keep my big girl panties on, and go to work with a good attitude, knowing I will learn from this. Right?

Evan gives me my keys, and tells me again, how lucky I am to work with him. What is it? I think at least ten times now. I get it, I'm working in *Evan's kingdom*, the God of hair! Wow! Here's a learning curve, blessing or curse? I get in my Volkswagon Rabbit. Ruth and I call it "the poor man's porche." I just feel like a fist is in my gut! I now have to go home, and I can't tell Juanita I think that her cousin is a jerk, to put it nicely! Oh, how I have waited to be 18 and in control of my life! This is not how I planned it! Well, I will call Ruth when I get home. She has a way of calming me down, or making me laugh. Sometimes, all we need is a good laugh, and that changes our atmosphere.

I'm pulling in the drive, and feel relieved, Juanita and Jack are gone. I don't have to act like all is well, when I feel like running back home! Ouch! I can't believe I just thought that, when I've waited my whole life to be 18 and on my own! I hope Ruth is home, I sure do need to vent! The phone just rings, no answer! Ok. I'll call my big sis, she is always a calm in my storm! "Hey sis!" "Oh hey, how is life in the mountains?" "Well I think

I may have made a mistake." "What do you mean?" "My boss is a self-absorbed jerk!" "How so?" She asks. "He talks to me, like I'm an idiot! Oh, and thinks it's okay to slap my ass! I am wondering if I made a mistake?" "Well I can't answer that, but I think you need to try it for a week and see, maybe?" "Well I wanted to be a big girl! I sure don't want Mom and Dad to hear this talk!" "Don't you worry, I won't say anything! I will tell you this, ask him if you were a man, would he be slapping your ass? I can tell you that answer, oh hell no!" We laugh! "Well I'm going to give it a try and see what happens." "I know you're going to be great, no matter what! Trust what you know, and have learned. You have great instincts and you are wise beyond your years! I have always told you that. You're awesome sis!" "So are you!" "Well, I have to get back to work, call me later if you need to. I'm always here for you." "Okay I will, love you." "Love you too!" "Bye". I hit the sister lottery! Thank you God! Now I need to hit the boss lottery! I laugh at myself. Good thing I think I'm funny. Well the good book says, laughter is like medicine to our soul. I'm thinking I'm going to need to overdose myself with it, to get through this!

Okay Hannah, get it together. You are going to work in the morning and you must have the right outfit! What to wear? I start pulling out clothes and the game begins! I'm on my fourteenth outfit! What is wrong with me, why can't I make a decision? So I begin to ponder, that I read one time, that millionaire's are people, that make decisions quickly. I need to work on that one, because that's my plan! I want to be a millionaire! Then, I could hire a person who could pick out the perfect outfit for me! Making myself laugh again. I suppose I'm learning to make friends with myself. I'm such a people person, and I come from a large family, so I have not had a lot of alone time. This is new, but I'm excited to learn about me. Ok. I have settled on my "painted on jeans" as my Mom calls them, with a sweater and my boots. It's a lot colder in the mountains, so this desert rat is going to have to learn a new dress code.

Oh, I hear Juanita and Jack coming up the stairs. "Hey!" Jack hollers. I holler back, "hey!" Here it comes, Juanita asks about my meeting with Evan. Well I lie, and say it was great! What she says next comes as a shock to me! "Really? That surprises me." I'm thinking, *what the hell?* So I answer her, "what do you mean?" She answers, "he is my cousin, but I think he is a male chauvinist ass!" Wow! I did not see that coming! I have a laugh, and she laughs! "So your meeting was not really okay, was it?" "Well, not exactly," I say. So I tell her all about it, and she lets me know that she is on my side. I cannot put into words my relief. This is my safe place after all! It's funny how we can decide how things will be. I had figured that I would have to lie to Juanita about Evan, and I was so wrong. We are so alike in our thinking, and I felt it from the moment I met her, so why did I not trust that? I think about my earlier conversation with my sister, *you have great instincts, trust what you know*. I'm learning.

Juanita wants to help me with Evan, and explains to me that she does not want to talk bad about him. But the truth is the truth, and he is hard to take at times. He is a great stylist, and so she encourages me to learn all that I can, and not put up with his B.S. I ask her why she did not say something earlier to me about him. She explains, that she did not feel like she should, because I was so excited about coming to Tall Pines. She also goes on to say, that it's important for me to learn, to make my own opinions, and she feels like Evan will teach me something. And it will be *my* choice what I do with it. I tell her I have a saying, "you can let life make you better or bitter." I don't know where I came up with it, but I claim it as a Hannah quote. "So I will let it make me better!" Jack walks in the room and says "Hannah you sure are lookin' purdy today!" Wow, he just stole my heart! I need him in the 20-year-old version! I'm feeling so blessed to be here with Juanita and Jack! Juanita tells me, that Jack will be going to his Dad's on Thursday, and wants to take me out Friday night to celebrate my first week in big girl panties! I'm in! What a day it's been, what will tomorrow bring? I'm feeling nervous, but I will think happy thoughts! I try on my work outfit for Juanita. She likes it, but accessorizes me with some of her jewelry. I'm having so much fun playing dress up! I'm feeling better about tomorrow. We eat the most delicious Mexican food, green enchiladas, with beans and rice. It's soul food for us, New Mexicans! Juanita has done it again! She is such a great cook. She is teaching me all of her secrets, so that one day I will win the stomach of my Prince Charming! "Don't they say, that the way to a man's heart is through his stomach?" Juanita says, "no girl, it's his pants!" Oh my, I'm learning!

I got the dishes done, and Jack wants me to read to him tonight. I love our story time, and it gives Juanita some much needed time to herself, as well. We settle on *The Giving Tree* and *Leo The Late Bloomer*. I love children's books! What a great story for me to hear. I want to remember to be happy where I'm at right now, and to not chase happiness. This world tells us, that if only you have *this* car, or house, body, face, boobs, man, woman you will be happy. It reminds me of chasing a dollar in the wind, as soon as you get to it, the wind blows it away again, and you keep chasing it! That is the lie the world tells us. Happiness is not a place or bank account, not that it is wrong to want good things, it's important to have goals! I just know that joy comes from God, and I can choose it daily. My worth, is not in what *man* labels me, it comes from being a child of God! Now don't get me wrong, I want money, a nice car and home. I believe as God's child I am to become all He made me to be, and to be excellent! I see money as a tool to bless with. Jack falls asleep, and I gently crawl out of his bed. Sweet dreams, Jack!

Washing my face and the phone rings, it's Ruth! "Hey there, how's it going?" "Well, it's been a crazy day! I tried to call you earlier for some comic relief!" "Really, what's up?" "Well my boss…I am feeling nervous about working with him." So I tell Ruth all about him, and she says, "well, you just have to stand up to him, and let him know you will not be treated like a dumb bimbo!" I start to laugh hard! "So that was not my dream to move away to become a dumb bimbo?" Ruth is laughing too! "Well," she says, "I guess that sounds a little harsh…but, you know what I am saying." "Oh, I totally get what your saying. Truth hurts! I just need to try it and see." I also share what Juanita said. Ruth says, "well Amen, you have her on your team!" "Yes, I am so happy about that!" "So how was your day?" "Well get ready for this…I'm going to beauty school!" "Wow! I was not expecting that, but you are always on top of the latest, greatest beauty things! I know you will be great!" "Well, we will see. I just don't feel a calling for anything else." I wonder about that… *is this my calling?* "We will see." I tell Ruth, "maybe, sometimes we think we are headed to our calling, and it is just going to be a stepping stone to get us there." She says, "I never thought about that. Oh, you are such a thinker! That's what I love about you! We are both analyzers of life. We love to listen to each other's thoughts, and don't always agree, but agree to laugh at ourselves!" "I miss you so much," I tell her. And she says "not more than I miss you!" "I hope you can come visit soon!" "Me too!"

"How's Jeff?" That is Ruth's boyfriend, that I'm not crazy about! "Oh he is good, he wants me to get a boob job." Oh, how it burns me up that he says that to her! She always has felt bad, because she has small breasts, and then he has to tell her that! "Tell him to kiss your perfect ass!" She laughs, and says, "oh, he just knows that I feel bad about my boobs." "Well, you know how I feel about it." "Yes I do! But you don't know Jeff the way I do." "You've got that right! I know he is always causing you to doubt yourself.

I'm sorry, I hate that. Your Mom does that to you too, and it just makes me crazy! You are such a great person, and I just can't stand when people try to create doubt in us, and make us feel like less. I mean Ruth, really, I feel like it's like that kid's book, *If you give a mouse a cookie*… well he will want a glass of milk, and so on. That's plastic surgery. So you get boobs, then you will want something else. I don't know, but I just want you to do it because you want it, not because the world, or Jeff told you, that you needed it to be good enough for a world stamp of approval. You are perfect!" I tell her. "Oh, if only everyone else could see me through your eyes!" "Well, what matters is that you see yourself through love. I struggle with that one too! If we could just see the beauty we see in each other!" "Well, thank God he put us together to remind each other, that we are princesses." "That's right! Now where is my prince charming?" "Have you met any cuties?" "Not yet. Juanita is taking me out on Friday so we will see." "Maybe you will find you a mountain man." We laugh. "I could use a rich one!" "Couldn't we all! So when do you start beauty school?" "I start in a week." "I loved it, I hope you have a fun bunch like I did." "Me too. Well I guess we better say goodbye, since I need to get to bed and get rested for my first day, as the dumb bimbo!" Laughter! "I needed to laugh, thank you for always making me find the funny!" "Oh well, maybe that's my calling." "Your right, it is. Sorry the pay is not better." "Well, make some money and put me on the payroll." "I'm on it!" "Ok, we must hang up, you know we can go on and on about silliness!" "Yes we can! Goodnight, love you." "Love you too! Mizpah!" "Mizpah!" That is something Ruth's Mom had us start. It means, "the Lord keeps you, and me, while we are apart."

Oh, Ruth's sweet Mama. She is such a good lady, but she speaks such negative over Ruth, and I just can't take it. She did not like me in the beginning, but I did not give up, and now she adores me. Well, I smoked, and she hated that. Can't blame the ol' girl! I don't know how many packs of cigarettes and lighters she threw away. I would forget, and leave them in my pocket, and she always checked my pockets when I would come in, and out they would go! Funny thing, I met Ruth walking into high school after being treated badly by my supposed to be "best friends," because the cute guy asked me out, and not any of them. I was not really interested in him, but said yes to be nice. Well, I was kicked out of the group! Broke my heart, I really thought they were my friends. But, God had a plan. He would put Ruth in my path and she would be my best friend, and my girl love. No, we are not gay, but if we were we would be a couple! Making myself laugh again! Anyhow, Ruth was smoking, and asked if I wanted one? I said sure, so that's how we started. I just let her Mom think I was the bad influence, as she said at first. It's funny how parents want to blame others for their children's bad choices. She knows the truth, but I think it's just easier for her to believe the lie. Well here's the thing, we are both on our journey and not trying to hurt anyone, but parents take it very personal. It seems as though *our* F is *their* F. Not true. But I will one day understand what they have gone through, when I have children myself, I hope. Of course I will do it *my* way, and better. Yeah, right! Oh Hannah, get to bed and quit analyzing things. Maybe I should have been a psychiatrist? Stop Hannah!

Settled into my bed, and hear go the voices of doubt! I hate it. So I begin to think of good things, and all my blessing, but they continue to creep in. I hear a voice that says, *what you focus on, is where you'll go*. Thoughts may come, but if they are not encouraging, let them go, and keep on letting them go, no matter how many times they come! I think how interesting our minds our. They sure can become a battlefield at times. I'm going to choose the voice of love, and get some sleep! I thank God, and peace falls over me, and rest follows.

CHAPTER 2

The Good, the Bad, and the Ugly

It's six-thirty in the morning, the alarm goes off. It's Jack's rooster alarm clock that he lent me. It's pretty funny that it actually says, "cock-a-doodle-doo, cock-a-doodle-doo." I lay in bed for a few moments thinking, what have I done? Oh, here comes doubt and worry! *Get up Hannah!* I say to myself. *You can do this, you have a license and everything you need.* Somehow, the dream is much different than the reality.

I shower, and spend thirty minutes on my hair. Thank goodness, I picked out my outfit yesterday. Ok, I'm feeling pretty good about myself. My hair looks good, outfit's good, I'm ready to do it! They say self talk is a good thing, so I continue to encourage myself and repeat aloud, "it's gonna be a great day, all is well!"

I head into the kitchen, and Juanita is getting Jack breakfast. I eat a quick bowl of cereal. Juanita is sweet to encourage me, and reminds me to not let Evan intimidate me. "I won't," I tell her. I'm such a people pleaser. *That is something I need to work on*, I think to myself. I want everyone to like me, and want to play with me. I get my stuff and head for my car. I want to be early. I want to get the feel of things, and set up my station before I start working this morning. Hoping to beat Evan there, and have a little alone time before *the king* arrives, I laugh at myself. *You're funny, Hannah!* Driving to work, I'm blown away again by the beauty that surrounds me. I can't believe I get to live here, so beautiful! Wow, there's a deer with a baby, there's two babies! Now, that's something I would never see back home. Ok, I better pay attention to my driving. I arrive, and there it is, *Evan's kingdom.* I'm going in!

Oh, thank goodness he's not here yet. I need to change my attitude! I get all my stuff out, a few things that I have, my scissors, my cape, the accessories a hairdresser needs. Well let's hope I get to do at least one customer today. Oh my, I see *the King* coming down the sidewalk. My stomach is in knots now, I feel like throwing up. This is not good, should I feel like this at the sight of my new boss? In he walks, first thing he says to me is, "you don't have a coffee going yet?" "Well no," I say, "I didn't know I was supposed to. I'm sorry." "Well get it going little girl!" Already called me little girl! "I don't really make coffee, so could you show me how you like it?" He says, "well I guess I'm going to have to show you everything!" He slaps me on the butt again. I am trying so hard to keep it together, I just want to run out of that building as fast as I can!

The King shows me how to make coffee, and just how he likes it. His first client comes in. She is an older woman, but well kept. Evan asks me… well *tells* me to shampoo her. I introduce myself to her and she says to me, "I'm Dorothy, and I hope that you can shampoo as good as Evan does, he's got the best hands!" Well I tell her, "I only hope that I can be, all that Evan is one day." Evan hears me, and hollers, "that's a big dream little girl!" Oh my goodness, if he calls me *little girl* one more time... I just want to scream! Well I don't, but I want to.

I begin a conversation with Dorothy, asking her what she does. She comes from money, she tells me, and she does as she pleases. She dabbles in several things. She owns a shoe store in town. "I do love shoes, you'll be seeing me." I tell her. She says to me, "you know Hannah, you're never disappointed by shoes, you'll never look at yourself and say, *do these shoes make me look fat?*" "You're right!" I laugh! "Now that's a good point… makes me love shoes even more!" Dorothy, then tells me she is also an artist. I tell her, that is something that I would love to try, "I love watercolors." She encourages me and says, "you never know what hidden talents are inside of you if you don't try." Now there's a golden nugget I'm going to hold onto. At first, I wasn't sure about Dorothy, but as we finish her shampoo I think to myself, *I really like her*.

As I listen to Dorothy's conversation with Evan, I love her comfort with having money. I think about how I grew up having plenty, but always felt guilty about it. We were not rich, I guess you would call us, "upper middle class." Whatever. I start to think about why that was my thought on money. Memories flood me of being told, *people were starving, money does not grow on trees, I grew up with nothing. We were lucky to have a banana, or an orange in our stocking at Christmas. You kids are spoiled brats!* So it hits me like a baseball bat against my head. I grew up always hearing things of guilt, and shame about money. And for having it, and being blessed. I will have to take this up with God, because I don't think he intended us to be blessed, and feel shame and guilt for it. Dorothy certainly does not.

I'm not saying that those things are not true, and did not happen, but do we need to keep playing the old record? Here I go, just as Ruth says, *I'm going to analyze it*. Well, I think, *if we are blessed, we are supposed to be a blessing!* Amen sister! Listen to me…oh well. *The King* is calling, and I must answer. I check Dorothy out, and she gives me a 25% off certificate for her shoe store, and gives me a five dollar bill for shampooing her. She also says to me, "Evan better watch out, you give a good shampoo!" I smile and say, "thank you!" "You ever need any pointers in business, you give me a call." I would love to hang out with Dorothy. My mother always said, *you are who you hang out with*. Here's the thing, I think I can learn a few things from Dorothy. I love that she didn't make me feel like I was beneath her in any way. The five dollar tip wasn't bad either, I sure wasn't expecting that! Dorothy has a generous spirit, that's what I want to be, a generous spirit.

Evan has been busy all morning, and I'm his go to girl. *Hannah get this!* And I get it. *Why haven't you done that already Hannah?* Well at least he hasn't called me *little girl* in awhile. I really am grateful for this job. I guess my attitude is, I just feel disrespected by him. But I will do as my good ol'Dad says, *to give them more than they expect, always do your best, and be the best! Treat it like it's your business*. I'm thinking back, and remembering how much I wanted to be a big grown-up girl! Oh sweet Hannah, careful what you pray for little girl!

Well it's lunchtime, and in walks Evan's girlfriend, Carrie. Wow, she looks nothing like I thought she would. Really, I don't know what I thought she would look like. She's really plain, simple, and her hair is really not that great. Well, she treats him like a *King*, so I get it. She's very kind and sweet, I can see that. It's funny how in the beginning, you don't find a person that attractive, and then you get to know them, and they become more beautiful. I see that about Carrie.

Well her and Evan are going out for lunch, so I will be in charge of the beauty shop. He didn't even mention me leaving for lunch, I guess it's a good thing I have some snacks in my car. So I run out to my car, grab my snacks, and wonder what Evan's policy is on eating in the beauty shop. Oh well, I'm going to eat because I'm starving! This consists of a *healthy*: Fritos, and half of a Payday candy bar. Makes me miss my Dad, he loves a Payday! I need to get some groceries, so I can make myself a lunch everyday. My chequing account is pretty sad! So as I'm *eating* my payday, I'm *thinking* I'm needing a pay day! Making myself laugh…kinda.

The phone rings, and it's a man. He wants a haircut. I ask him if he has a preference, and he simply answers, "no," he does not. He just needs a haircut today. I tell him I have a one-thirty available, he says he'll take it. He tells me his name is Harold, and he will see me shortly. As soon as I hang the phone up, I start jumping and shouting for joy, my goal is complete today, one haircut! So maybe I should've made a bigger goal, but hey it's a goal, and I'm going to complete it. Looking out the window I see *the King*, and Carrie pull up. They both look a little stressed. Well, not my business, I'm not going to worry about it. I just hope he is not in a bad mood for the rest of the day!

In walks *the King*, and he is not in a good mood. *It's gonna be a long afternoon in the beauty shop.* So here goes the middle child, let's try to make this guy happy again. I share right away that I have a haircut coming at one-thirty. Evan says, "yeah well, you better not screw it up." "Well alrighty then, that's encouraging!" So I wasn't feeling nervous, but now I'm really nervous! So this is like the third time today I want to throw up. Well, in-walks one of Evan's buddies, so I have a reprieve. He's cutting his hair, and I'm going to my little work space.

It's one-fifteen, and in walks my haircut, Harold. He is an older gentleman, bald on top, and only has white hair on the sides and back of his head, so this should be an easy haircut. I'm feeling better, I think I'm going to make it. So I take Harold to the shampoo bowl and shampoo his hair, well what little he has. I'm shampooing him and I think, *how hard is it on men to lose their hair?* I don't think I'll ask Harold about that today. So I walk Harold back to my chair, and I begin to cut his hair. He asks me where I'm from, so I tell him my story. He begins to share with me, that he remembers when the road from Tall Pines to my hometown, was just a one lane dirt road. "Wow, that's crazy," I tell him, "I can't imagine." He says, "well young lady, when you've lived as long as I have, there's lots to tell." "I bet that's right," I say.

It's all going well, until I cut my finger! I can't get it to quit bleeding! I run it under the water, and Harold tells me to apply pressure, so I do. I don't want Evan to know this! Oh my goodness Hannah, why did you cut pass that second knuckle? You know the rules. I think I've got the bleeding under control, so I start cutting Harold's hair again. I begin to bleed again, it's getting all over Harold's hair. His hair is now pink instead of white. Oh, I want to die right now! Please, please don't let Evan come around the corner. I'm telling Harold how sorry I am, he says, "oh, calm down. If this is the worst thing that happens, we will be okay honey." Thank you God, for this kind man. I just wish this was not happening right now.

Oh no, I hear Evan coming around the corner. He takes one look and says, "what in the world?" I say, "well I cut my finger." "I see that," he says. "Why are you bleeding all over this poor man?" "I tried to stop it, and I just can't get it to stop. Every time it stops, I start to cut his hair, and it starts bleeding again." Evan tells me to go in the bathroom, and wash my finger off to try to get the bleeding to stop, and he'll finish the haircut. Well sweet little Harold says, "sir that won't be necessary, she can finish my haircut, I'm in no hurry." So Evan gives me the dirtiest of looks, "just get the bleeding stopped before you continue his haircut, and wash his hair again." *Duh, like I wasn't going to.*

So now I'm really questioning my decision to become a hairstylist. I finish Harold's haircut, and he tells me I did a great job. I'm so thankful for the kindness and patience Harold showed me. I will remember, and pass it on when I have the chance. Evan has had a busy afternoon, I'm grateful I have not had to deal with him much, except to be his go get this, *go get that girl*, but I can deal with that. There's only thirty minutes left until I get to leave, hallelujah!

Oh, what a day. I'm thinking of quitting, but I don't think it's really an option at this point. I will take the good, the bad, and the ugly, and learn from it. Really, all the people I encountered, except for my boss, were pretty wonderful! My grandmother would always say to me, "child, you have a basket full of beautiful apples, and you're focusing on the one bad one, so get over it!" Life is getting real, quick!

CHAPTER 3

My Angels

So I'm two months into working at Evan's kingdom. I continue to stay focused on the basket of good apples, but that one bad apple… wow it sure can mess with you. It's been rough trying to pay my rent, and I had to take on a few side jobs, here and there just to make it. I'm excited today, I have three new clients! Pulling into work and determined to stay positive, I walk into the shop, and Evan's already there. I say, "well good morning, how was your weekend?" His reply, "what are you so dang happy about?" I think, *really? Already?* Oh well, I'm not going to let him suck me into his drama. "Well, I have three new clients today!" He surprises me with "well good for you."

Good deal, it's half-past nine, and in walks my first client. Her name is Sue. Sue had asked me if she could bring her special needs son, Weston, and I said of course. So behind Sue is Weston, a big kid with a great smile, and curly blond hair. He immediately puts his hand out and says, "hi I'm Weston." I say, "well how do you do Weston? I am Hannah, and I'm so glad to meet you." He then says, "you're pretty, Hannah." "Thank you very much Weston." Sue tells me, he is a ladies man. I show Weston where he can sit. We go to the shampoo bowl, and I begin to wash Sue and talk to her about her hair. So today we will give her a perm and haircut, and she'll be back next week for color. "Wow I'm excited!"

I really like Sue, she's positive, and full of joy. I really needed this apple today. So as I'm rolling her hair, we begin to have a talk about her life. She has two children, her daughter Catherine, and Weston. And she starts to tell me Weston's story. So I carefully listen, as she explains that she did not know that he would be born with down syndrome. So it was a surprise, she then tells me, that many of her friends were pregnant at the same time, and all of them gave birth to healthy babies. It was hard at first, she explains. She says, "you know, it's kind of like you're packed to go on a trip to Italy, and all your friends are going to Italy, and then they tell you, *oh I'm sorry you're not on the plane for Italy, you're going to Holland.* But I packed for Italy, and you're not ready for Holland. Everything you have is for Italy, you don't know anything about Holland. I was grieving Italy, I woke up one day and realized I'm missing the beauty of Holland because I'm so focused on not going to Italy. That is when I changed my attitude about Weston and I began to see all the beauty of Holland. The things that he would teach me that Italy would have never taught me. You see Hannah, we always have a choice, there is always beauty if we choose to see that beauty. I'm not saying that it's not hard sometimes, but even life in Italy is hard sometimes. I do, at times wish I could just drop off Weston at the pool, like the other Mother's do, but I can't. So I will just have to find the best black bathing suit I can, for the rest of my life." Oh my, what a blessing for me today to hear that story. That one will forever change me.

Finished up Sue's hair, and she loves it! Weston is funny, he's a "bull in a china shop," as Sue puts it. Everything he does, he does it big! I hate that our time is over. I just love Sue and Weston, and can't wait to see them next week. Well, I hope my next two clients are as good as them. I think the hardest thing about my job is having to switch over for the next personality. You have to figure out what they need, and it isn't always just about their hair.

I clean up my mess, and Evan's mess too. I'm feeling a little funny, like I'm getting sick. *No! I don't have time or money for it!* My next client shows up thirty minutes early to look at hair books. She is a really cute girl, I hope I can give her what she wants. I introduce myself to her, and she says "*nice to meet you,*" in a real southern accent. I tell her how much I like her accent, and she says, "I hate it! I have been gone from the south for years, but can't lose it." "Well I like it, it makes you, you! It's funny," I tell her, "I don't think I have an accent, but spent a summer back east and people would ask me about my accent. *I don't have an accent*, I would say. *Oh yes you do*, they would reply." "Well," she says, "I would gladly trade you."

I sit Katie down in my chair, and we begin to discuss her hair. She has no idea what she wants, she just wants a change. Danger, I hate that! I get it, sometimes we feel stuck in life and the only thing we feel we can change, is our hair. That can be *really* good or it can be *really* bad! Good news, she has great hair! We settle on a cute shag. As I'm cutting her hair, she begins to share her problems with her boyfriend. So I just listen to her. I start to want to fix it for her, but something stops me and says, *listen, just listen to her*. And for a change, I listen to that voice. And I *did* just listen, and realized, that what she needed was just somebody to hear her. We finish her hair, and it does look really cute. I was proud of myself, and Evan even came in and complimented me on the haircut. *Hey, there's a miracle*. Katie says, "I feel like I've known you forever, you are just the best. I'm so glad I found you!" Wow, all I did was listen. We hug, and Katie's on her way, with a new attitude and a new haircut. Miracles do happen in the beauty shop.

So far, so good today! I just wish I was feeling better. I have one more to go, the day is going fast. Evan has been nice today, *kind of scary!* I laugh to myself. I'm staying positive. My last client is late, I hope she shows up. I'm counting on that money today. That is something I am realizing, a lot of people don't really understand when they miss appointments. Yes, we can reschedule them, but we are out that money and time. I understand most of the time we don't get that, unless we live somebody else's life. A lot of people charge, if you miss your appointment. I'm just not sure how I feel about that yet. Well so far, she's ten minutes late, how long should you give the person? I'm wondering, so I ask Evan. He says that he gives them fifteen minutes, unless he is pushed for time, then he reschedules them. "Ok." I tell him, "well I'm not pushed for time, and I need the money, so I'm gonna give her more time, I hope she shows."

I'm feeling worse by the minute, but I see a woman walking up the sidewalk, maybe it's Wilma. *She has the biggest hair I've ever seen, oh my goodness!* She walks in the door and says, "hi there, my name is Wilma. I'm here to see Helena." It's my client, only twenty minutes late. "Hello, my name is *Hannah*." She says, "oh, sorry, I thought it was Helena." "Well it's nice to meet you Wilma, come on back and we'll get started."

So, Wilma begins to tell me all about her hair. She likes it ratted as tall, and as big as you can get it! She's a hoot! "And I want it dyed jet black," and likes the sides "winged back" as she puts it. She has a really pretty face, and cute figure. She kind of reminds me of Dolly Parton in a way. We get started on her color. She tells me she's sorry for being late, but she is a waitress, and lunch was crazy today, "people are so messy! We had extra clean up to do." I tell her, she was my last client of the day.

So we get Wilma's hair dye on, and I sit and visit with her, as her hair is processing. She also grew up in the south, Birmingham Alabama. Married her childhood sweetheart, they've been in love ever since. "Oh girl, we have the best sex!" Ok here's the deal, we are not the only one's in the shop. Evan has two customers, one man waiting for him, and a lady getting her hair done. I guarantee, she said it so loud, they probably could hear next door. She has one of those voices that carries, and there is no soft to it. So funny! She then tells me, that last Christmas, she fixed her hair all up and did her makeup, and was naked under the Christmas tree with just a red bow on top when her man came home from work. "I don't know if I told you, but he's a fireman." I said, "no, you did not. Lucky man to have you!" "Well," she said, "I think we should do our best to keep it spicy!" "I will keep that in mind when I find my man." "You mean to tell me a cute little thing like you, don't have a man yet?" "No, not yet," I tell her. She makes me sound pitiful! "Well, I thank the good Lord for giving me my man for all these years! Honey, by your age, I had been with my Charlie for seven years." Wow! "Well how about you ask the Lord to send my man." "You really want me to?" "Well, yes!" "Ok then, get ready 'cause when I pray, the mountains move!" I love her faith! "I will get ready," I tell her. "You think I'm kidding you?" "Oh no ma'am, I know you're telling me the truth." The timer goes off, and we rinse her hair and trim it. "Not too much," she says, "I need it to be high and wide!"

"My Charlie says, *honey you got that hair touching Heaven!* And I say, *Charlie, haven't you ever heard the bigger the hair, the closer you are to God?*" I laugh, I've never heard that, but I'll use it. "That's another thing honey, besides keeping things spicy in the bedroom, you got to have a sense of humor. Charlie says, I can just make him madder than anything, then I turn around and do something to make him laugh, that's why he loves me. I finish her hair up and we begin to style it. Here's where the problem is, I don't know if I'm going to be able to get it high and wide enough! I'm starting to feel really bad, and kind of feverish. I'm ratting like a crazy woman. I just can't get it to stay in, the way she wants it. She takes the comb from me, and she starts ratting her hair, saying, "just get it in there, tight as you can. I like big, don't be afraid." One hour later, she is touching heaven! Hallelujah!

I check her out as she says to me, "you did pretty good for your first time. I'll be back to give you another try. I'll have to call to re-schedule, I don't know what my work schedule will be like. Get ready for your man, girl!" "I will! Thank you Wilma!" "By the way, are you okay? You're not looking so good." "I'm feeling a little funny," I say. "Well get home and rest." "I will. Good night!" Oh, how I wish I could skip clean up!

I pull into the drive, Juanita and Jack are getting out of their car. Juanita tells me, Jack is not feeling well, he is running a fever. "He is not the only one." "You too?" she says. "Yes me too! Do you need any help getting anything out of the car?" "No I've got it." I take Jack's small hand and say, "come on buddy, let's go in the house and get warm." "It is freezing, Hannah!" "You've got that right, buddy!" I have nothing to take for this, but luckily Juanita has a few things. She drugs Jack and I up, and off to bed we go. She says, "I don't know who is more pitiful out of you two." Jack says, in his sweet little voice, "I'm the mostest sick." "I'll let you win this one bud. Love you! Get better!" "I love you too, Hannah." Oh that melts my heart.

I'm laying in bed thinking, *what if I don't feel better in the morning?* I do have only one haircut in the morning. Although I feel horrible, I thank God for my day, and the people sent to bless me. I fall asleep replaying the day. Sweet sleep, please!

Oh no, the rooster is crowing! It can't be time to get up already, I'm not better! Juanita is talking to Jack. She knocks, and asks how I'm feeling. "Not good," I report. "Jack is still running a temperature." "I think I am too." Juanita says, she is going to take Jack to the doctor. "Do you want an appointment?" "Well, how much is it?" I ask. "If you're sick Hannah, you need to go." "My money is tight." "I'll lend you money." "Oh, I can't do that, you have enough to take care of…I guess make me an appointment. I need to call Evan. I am not looking forward to this." "What are you supposed to do?" Asks Juanita, "you're sick." "I know, but you know how Evan is. Yesterday he was in a pretty good mood, and he actually complimented me on a haircut. So I'll pray that he's in that mood today." Here it goes, I dial Evan's number. Ring, ring, ring. Finally he answers, "hello?" "Hey Evan, it's Hannah, I'm calling because I'm sick. I was feeling bad yesterday evening, but I'm really sick today, and so is Jack." "So, what are you saying to me? You're not coming to work today?" "Well I have a haircut this morning. What do you think I should do, should I cancel it?" "I don't know what you should do, you're not a little girl, figure it out. I have a crazy day, and I really needed you to be there today." "Well, I'm sorry but I don't think you want to be around me with this. I will try to call my haircut and figure it out. I'm sorry Evan, I'm gonna go to the doctor, so hopefully I can be in there tomorrow." "Alright, let me know what you're doing, bye!"

I break down in tears. "I know I'm sick, I want my mom, and I just want to go home!" Juanita gives me a hug, and tells me it will be alright. "I know, I just am not sure I want to be around a person that is so negative, and mean most of the time." "Hey, you can't make him better if he won't choose it. I think you have done great, staying this long. Let's get you a doctors appointment, and get you better. Then you can decide what to do about work." "You're right, things always seem much worse when you feel bad." I try to call my haircut, and don't get an answer. So I tell Juanita, "don't make my appointment until after eleven o'clock, I have to go do a haircut." "Are you kidding me? You're gonna do the haircut?" "I have to, I can't get a hold of him, and Evan is no help!" "Okay then, I'll see if they can get you in after eleven."

I head for the shower to get ready for work. I ask God to give me strength to get through this day. I do it! I get dressed! That felt like an Olympic sport! Juanita tells me, that I have a one o'clock appointment with the doctor. She explains where the office is. She also asks me, if I can watch Jack when I get home from the doctor. I say "sure, we can be pitiful together."

I head for work and walk in, to *Mr. Happy!* He hardly speaks. I just go past him, into my little space. In-walks my haircut. Oh, he is cute! I so wish I looked, and felt better! He says, "hey there, my name is Ben, I have a haircut with Hannah." "That's me!" "Great," he says. "Come on back and I'll shampoo you. I tried to call you, but no answer." "Oh sorry, I leave my house at six for work...well I was still sleeping then. Why did you call?" "I woke up not feeling great." "Oh, bummer!" "Yeah, it is. I was going to see if we could change your appointment." "Do you want to do this another time?" "No, I'm good with it if you are. I just don't want to give, whatever this is, to you."

I shampoo Ben's hair, he tells me that it's his favorite part of this whole process, "I love getting my hair shampooed." *That's just cute*, I think to myself. He tells me how he wants his hair cut. While I'm cutting his hair, he asks me where I'm from, and how long I've been in Tall Pines. I share my story, and ask him his. He has his own construction company. He is young, and thinking to have his own company. *Well he certainly has it together.* He asks me if I like dancing. "Yes, I love dancing! I'm not a great country dancer, but would love to learn. How about you?" "I'm ok I guess, I like doing it though. Maybe when you heal up, we could go dancing." "That would be great!" I finish his haircut and he pays me, and gives me a ten dollar tip! I tell him that's too much, "you're haircut was only eight bucks!" He says, "yeah, but anybody that comes to work sick, deserves a ten buck tip! So thanks! Can I get your number, and call you sometime?" "Sure," I write it on a piece of paper, hand it to him, and off Ben goes.

I am cleaning up my mess, and remember what Wilma said to me, about *praying for me, a man.* That was quick! I better call and tell her to pray for me to get well! I tell Evan I'm leaving and he just mumbles, "bye." *Really? That's all ya got for me?*

• • •

I pull up to the doctor's office, glad that I'm here. Feeling worse by the minute, I sign in and they call me quickly. Dr. Mac walks in. He's tall, with a thick moustache, and hair that any girl would be jealous of. "Hello Hannah, I'm Dr. Mac." "Hi Dr. Mac." He is very nice, and makes me feel cared about right away.

Dr. Mac looks down my throat, and in my ears, takes my temperature, and says "young lady, you are one sick girl, you got a bad case of tonsillitis! You are going to need antibiotics, and I'm also going to give you a shot in the butt." No, not that! A shot of penicillin… my gosh, that's like putting peanut butter in a syringe with a hot needle! I'm not looking forward to this! Plus, I had only enough money for the appointment, and now I've gotten a shot, plus I need antibiotics. I prayed to be a big girl, can I change my mind God?

The nurse gives me my shot, ouch! To think, I could be buying a cute outfit for all of this. The truth is, I just want to feel good again. I'll wear my old clothes, just let me get better. The shot is over, and I go to the front to pay, and get my prescription. They tell me the best place to get it is across the street from the hospital. I get to my car and I think, *oh God, what am I gonna do?* I just used all the money I have, to pay the doctor, and now I need antibiotics too. I drive over to the pharmacy, and walk in. He looks up at me and says, "wow, you look like shit!" I say, "thank you, I feel like shit!" "What can I do for you?" I hand him the paper with my prescription on it. "Oh you are sick." "Sir, can I ask you to tell me first how much it will be? I'm not sure if I have enough money to pay you, and I don't want you to fill it if I can't pay for it."" Well first of all, I'm Dan, nice to meet you Hannah." "Nice to meet you Dan." Then he says, "we are going to open you a charge account here." "You can do that?" I ask. "I can do anything I want, I own the place." "That is so awesome! You're my hero!" "Well, that was easy."

As I wait for him to fill my prescription, a woman walks in, she's pretty and has a spunk to her. I don't know her, but would like to. She says to Dan, "how's it going?" "Great!" he answers. "How about you, Carla?" "Oh you know me, Dan, I'm always great, unless I'm not." Laughter! "Let me finish getting Miss Hannah fixed up, and I'll help you." "No problem, you know I love looking around your place. I will find something I don't need."

Carla walks over to me, and asks, "are you a hairdresser?" "Yes, I am, how did you know?" "Oh, you know, small town. But I've heard good things about you Hannah." "Well that makes me feel better." "So you're working for Evan, aren't you?" "Yes I am." "How's that going for you?" "Well I love my clients so far." "I hear you." Not sure what she meant by that. "Hey, I would love to take you to lunch sometime, or take you out for a drink in the evening." "That sounds fun." "Come by my shop sometime. It's on Main, downtown. I'm thinking of adding on to it. It's called *The Hair Tamer*." "I will, as soon as I'm better." Dan calls me, and I sign my charge. He hands me my medicine, I thank Dan again, and tell him and Carla how wonderful it was to meet them. I head for home! Bed is calling! As I'm driving, I think about how Dan was an angel for me today, and I wonder if Carla could be my angel too?

CHAPTER 4

The Silver Lining

Well it's been ten days, and I finally feel better. I guess I didn't realize how much stress I'm under, around Evan's negativity. I have to go back to work today, and I'm not looking forward to seeing Evan, but need to make some money. He never even checked on me, except to guilt trip me about missing work. Well, my Mom said that *he can only guilt you, if you let him.* She's right!

Ben called me last night, and wants to take me out dancing on Friday night. I started to wonder if he was going to call me. Well, it would not have done much good if he did, I haven't felt like doing anything until today. So, there is a rainbow at the end of my week. I kind of have that butterfly feeling, just thinking about it. Makes me a little nervous, too!

I finish getting dressed for work. The good news, I lost five pounds! Juanita said, "you didn't need to." I guess not, but for some reason, women struggle with thinking that they are okay with where they are. I walk into work, and Evan says to me, "well hello, I'm Evan and who are you?" So I play along, and say, "I'm your long lost friend." "Well," he says, "my friend better get to work." "Ok, I'm on it!" That was not so bad. I do some cleaning and fold towels, which is ongoing. I look out the window, and I see Dorothy walking up the sidewalk. *Yes, that's a great way to start the day! With a generous spirit!* "Well, good morning all you good people!" "Good morning Dorothy, how are you?" "Could not be better!" "That's great news. You know what's even better news?" "What?" I ask. "We are having a 50% off shoe sale!" "Oh, I love me a shoe sale! But, sad news is I can't make it. I was off work sick for ten days, and the bank account suffered greatly!" "That is sad news, sorry to hear you were sick." "Thanks Dorothy!"

Evan tells me to get Dorothy shampooed, so I take her back to the shampoo bowl. She asks me if I would be interested in helping her, she need some extra help at the shoe store. I say, "yes that would be great!" She also says, "you know, you can meet quite a few people, and give out your card's, and get your clientele going that way." "Oh Dorothy, thank you so much, you're always so helpful!" Then she says to me, "let me tell Evan, I'll work this out for you. Don't you worry, honey." "You're my hero Dorothy, I want to be just like you when I grow up!" "Oh, you're sweet Hannah, you are like me, you just have to grow into your rich-self. You must know Hannah, money is only a part of being rich, you want to be rich in every area of your life. We are, each of us, to ignite possibility in one another. You dear, are to dwell in possibility, always. Believe me, I see you! You are special!"

That would be something that would stick with me for the rest of my life. Dorothy saw me, when I could not see myself at that moment. For that, I will be forever grateful to her. What she shared that day with me, would impact my life in so many ways that I would never even realize, until much later.

Here's the thing that I could not understand, how did she not see and feel Evan's negativity? I guess she did, but did not let it affect her. She only had to deal with it in small doses, unlike me. One of the things I realize is, women will let a male hairdresser get away with a lot more than a female. I don't get it, but I have watched it in beauty school, and now with Evan. Sometimes he will run behind, and they will sit and wait on him for an hour or longer. Not the case for me, although I try really hard to not do that. I find it rude to not be considerate of other people's time. We even had a talk about that in beauty school, so I know it's not just my opinion.

Sue and Weston will be in shortly. I had to cancel her appointment and make her a new one since I was sick, she was quite kind about it. *I can't wait to see them!* Evan finishes Dorothy, and says to me, "so I hear you're going to help Dorothy out." "Yes, I need the extra money. I guess I was a bit naïve about becoming a hairdresser, I didn't realize how long it would take to build a clientele, and be able to pay my bills." "Well missing a week, did not help you." "Yeah I know." "Just make sure you keep your priorities straight." "I will." Dorothy comes out of the restroom, gives me a hug, and tells me to come by the shoe store after work today, and we would figure out a schedule for me. "Ok, I will be there." I'm excited to be around Dorothy, and to understand the truth of being rich.

In walks Sue and Weston. Weston comes up to me and gives me a big ol'Weston hug, then announces he missed me! "Well ok then, Mr. Weston." Sue says, "the beauty with him, is that you never have to guess how he feels." "Yes!" I say, "and that is refreshing." "Can be," Sue smiles. "So what are you thinking of your color?" "I don't want any big change, just want some shine. I feel like it looks dull, but I am loving my perm." "Oh good! Ok, here is what I'm thinking, we just got in some new color gloss, and I'm dying to try it! Ha! No pun on dying. It's more conditioning, leaves the hair really shiny, healthy looking, and feeling." "Alright," Sue says, "that sounds perfect."

I get her gloss on, and put her under the dryer. Weston is busy with a game he brought. The phone rings, and I answer, "Evan's hair kingdom!" I say, "oops! I mean hair shop." I hear laughter on the other end. "Hello, hey" she says, "is this Hannah?" "Yes it is, can I help you?" "Yeah, this is Carla." "Oh hey Carla! I was going to call, or come by and see you. I just came back to work today." "Oh my, you really were sick!" "Yes I was, don't want that again!" "Well, glad to hear you're better. I was calling to see if I could borrow a perm from you until my order comes tomorrow." "I don't see why not, but have to check with Evan. Hold on." "Hey Evan, it's Carla from *The Hair Tamer*, she wants to borrow a perm until tomorrow." "I guess." "Ok Carla, come get it." "I'll be right over, thanks!" "See ya soon!"

In walks Carla, oh my, she has a different color of hair this time. I say, "wow, your hair is a different color!" "Well I am a hairdresser, that's the fun of it, I get to have whatever color of hair I want. My husband says, he never knows who he is going to bed with." We laugh! I think of Wilma and keeping it spicy. I really like Carla's spunk! Evan says hello to her, and goes about his business. I give her the perm, and she says she will return tomorrow. "Well if you can't get here, I would be glad to stop and pick it up on my way home." "Ok, we will see what works."

She walks out and Evan turns to me, "you don't need to be picking anything up! If she borrows, then she brings it back." "Ok, I just thought I would be nice, it's on my way home." "Just mind your business Hannah, and I'll deal with the shop business." "Ok."

Sue's dryer stops, and I rinse her hair. "Wow!" she says, "I love how soft it feels." We dry it, and the color is perfect! "I knew you would do it perfect, Hannah!" "Thank you Sue, for your confidence in me. I'm still working on that part." "We are all a work in progress." "Why do I feel like, sometimes it's just me?" "We all do. What you need to know, is you just need to run Hannah's race! There is no competition, but yourself Hannah. I will tell you something, put yourself around people that encourage you in your race and not people who want to compete with you. People that create, will encourage you, people that compete, will try to keep you feeling like you are always behind. Don't fall for that! You're a winner, just ask Weston." "Am I a winner Weston?" "YES!" "Ok! I believe!"

That really is the truth, you have to believe you're a winner! "I'm so happy to have you, and Weston in my life. I don't know what I did to deserve you guys, but I'm grateful." "You are a good person, and that's what you're gonna bring into your life. Oh, there will be some bad apples occasionally, but they are just there to remind us of the beautiful apples, and all of our blessings. So don't lose focus of the good. I will share something that I learned years ago, when I'm having one of those days I sit down, and I write a list of all the good, and then I write a list of all the bad, or the hard stuff. I will tell you, you'll always feel blessed afterwards, knowing that the good always outweighs the bad." "My Grandma and Dad have always made me do that, Sue. That's who taught me, my Dad and Grandma." "Good teachers! See, already a *good* for your list. Remember dear, it's always darkest before the light! Here is something for you to do before bed every night, I have a little notebook by my bed and I simply write five things I'm grateful for that day." "That is a great idea! I will start tonight! You will definitely be on my list to Sue!" "Well, you'll be on mine, sweet girl!" I love when she calls me sweet girl! It's a little thing, but makes me feel super special!

"Ok, Mr. Weston and I have groceries to buy, so let's go son." "Bye Hannah!" "Bye Weston!" "I will call you, for my next appointment soon!" "Ok, thank you Sue, for everything!" "No, thank you! Remember, gratitude changes everything!"

I'm grateful! Even though Evan is hard to deal with, I would not have met Sue, Weston, and Dorothy if I were not here.

So there's the silver lining on the cloud of Evan, *The King*. Finishing up my chores for the day, sweeping, mopping and laundry. Could I be Cinderella? Only my story is different, I have only one wicked step-brother! *Thank goodness there is not three*. That can go on my good list! That thought makes me chuckle.

• • •

I'm excited, I got two calls from people who had been referred to me from previous clients! Of course I tried to share this with Evan, but the poor guy just can't be happy for me. I don't get it. Oh well, I'm going to focus on my silver lining. I get to go meet with Dorothy in a little while. I am going to have to be careful, I think to myself. Shoes? That's a weakness for me. I need money, not shoes right now. *God give me strength!* I'm laughing to myself. Ruth always says, she thinks it's funny how I ask God about all things, even shoes. Well I have told her, he says he cares about everything, so I figure he cares as much about the small things, as he does the big things. But Ruth tends to think that we really should not bother God for small things, we should just go to him with the big, giant things! That's where we disagree, but it's fine, we always say we can agree to disagree. In the church I grew up in, we had to go to confession and tell our sins to a priest. I never did feel right with that. I'm not saying that others should not do it, it just did not feel right in my spirit. If God knows all things, then he already knows my sins. So why do I need to go and tell a man, and then he tells me to do all these prayers and things to be right with God? I feel I can just go straight to him with my sin. I ask, "what about Jesus?" He said, "He came to finish what we can't." So I'm forgiven! I'm going to stick with that, because it feels right in my spirit. I shared that with my parents, and my Dad said, "well you have a valid point, so I guess you don't have to do confession, if it does not feel right to you." Thank you God, they listened! *Oh Hannah, where does your mind go girl?* I wonder if everybody does this? My mind will wander! Get your mind back to work, Hannah!

Okay I went to church for a minute there, I'm done. "Evan, is there anything else you need me to do before I leave?" "I guess not." "Ok then I'll see you tomorrow, have a good night." "Ok, see you tomorrow."

• • •

I pull into Dorothy's shoe store, so excited! "Hey there, sweetheart!" This is already a breath of fresh air. Sweetheart, wow! "Hey Dorothy, I'm so happy to be here, you don't know how grateful I am to you for this opportunity!" "Well back at you, Hannah! I'm equally grateful to have you! So I would say we are off to a good start!" I think to myself, *wow she's grateful to have me, I wish Evan felt like that!*

"So I'm gonna show you around, and also show you how I want you to do things. If you have any questions please ask, there are no dumb questions Hannah, remember that!" "Ok I will." Dorothy is so kind and patient, she really takes time to explain everything to me and fill me with confidence. I'm so very excited about this new opportunity, and then she tops it off with, "and you're always gonna have a discount on shoes here, I will let you charge it and only take $10 out of each check, per time." I want to scream, bingo! Of course I don't, but I think the smile on my face says it all. So I will work for Dorothy two half-days a week, and on Mondays. She has insisted that I have one day off, and that is Sunday. I told her I would work, and she said "Hannah, I'm teaching you to be rich, and in order to be rich in all things, you must have a day of rest!" "Ok Dorothy, you're the boss!" "You're a quick learner, Hannah!" "Thank you," I say. "How about I treat you to dinner." "I would love that Dorothy, but you don't have to treat."

"Miss Hannah, I want you to listen to me carefully, I want to treat you to dinner. It is a gift for me to give, and for you my dear, just receive gratefully. Your day will come to treat. There are times in our lives, Hannah, that we are the givers, and there are times that we are the receivers. No matter the time, we must do each, with gratitude." "I will accept with gratitude, Dorothy!" "That's my girl! Let's meet at Lilly's." So I follow Dorothy to the restaurant. I tell her I've never eaten here. She says, "well you're in for a treat, because it's delicious." The truth is, I could never afford to come to this restaurant right now, and Dorothy knows that.

I just want to pinch myself right now, I am feeling so blessed! I cannot believe, that this incredible woman wants to be my friend! We look at the menu, and Dorothy tells me to order whatever I want! She suggests the filet mignon. "That's what I was thinking of having, that sounds fabulous to me." "Oh, you won't be disappointed, it will melt in your mouth." We order, and then begin to visit. She asks me how things are going at the beauty shop. "It's going well, I'm starting to get return customers which is exciting! So far, the people have been really wonderful and patient, and kind." "I'm happy for you Hannah, you're gonna do well, you just have to hang in there and don't give up. What about Evan?" "What do you mean?" "I know he is not the most encouraging person you have around." "Well, that is true Dorothy. I don't want to speak badly about him, I just really don't know what to think about him. I could use some of your advice and wisdom about Evan." "I thought you would never ask!" Laughter! "Ok then, let it fly!" "Well here is the thing Hannah, it is not about you. Evan is an insecure man, and he wants you to feel insecure and doubt yourself." "Well you could fool me, all he tells me is how great he is and how lucky I am to work with him! In the months that I have been with him, he has given me one compliment on a haircut I did. I have hung on to that golden moment for survival!" "Oh Hannah, the man or woman who needs to be boastful, is secretly doubtful and afraid. We are created in God's image, therefore we are to create. We are not to compete, and Evan I'm afraid, does not get that. He is allowing selfish gratification to make you feel, that you are under his power and rule. You see, it is his problem, but the problem for you my dear, is to learn to determine who and what influences you want in your life."

"That is so true Dorothy, and I don't really know what to do about Evan. I go home every evening thinking about that very question. I don't know that I want his influence in my life daily, but I feel stuck. Plus, it's not all bad. I mean, without being there, I would not have met you, and so many other wonderful people." "And that is all true Hannah, that's what I love about you, you're always looking for the 'golden treasure.' But that does not mean that you have to sacrifice your beliefs, and what you know to be true and right for yourself. I am not gonna tell you what to do, but I will encourage you to consider what you feel in your spirit."

"I just don't know what I would do, Dorothy." "You just need to make the decision Hannah, and things will fall into place." "Well it feels scary to me Dorothy." "Well, sweet girl I've heard you talk of faith, and your belief in God, now is the time to exercise that. Faith is believing, without seeing it yet. See what you want, share that with God, and trust him for that of which you want." "You're right Dorothy! I want a boss that is grateful and encouraging like you...well I have one already, I do work for you now!" "Oh you do make me smile, Hannah! I just know it's all going to be good for you. I know your time with Evan has been hard, but sometimes our hardest experiences, are our greatest teachers if we just let them teach." "I do want to always choose to be better Dorothy." "I know you do child. Now I don't want you worrying about things. Just pray and consider."

"Okay," I tell her, "I will, I promise." We finish up dinner, I tell Dorothy she was right, the filet mignon was amazing! "I cannot thank you enough for this evening Dorothy, thank you for your wisdom and your generosity always." "Oh it has been my pleasure Hannah, I have enjoyed this time with you. I look forward to more time with you at the shoe store, the two of us will have a good time." "Oh I don't doubt that." I asked Dorothy one more question, "what has been your key to success?" She answers me with, "this, what I want for myself, I want for everyone else.

I get home, Juanita and Jack are not here. I remember, Juanita said they were going to meet Jack's Dad for dinner. I am tired after my day, and decide to get ready for bed.

Before getting into bed, I go over my day. I get out my little journal, and I begin to write the five things that I'm grateful for today as Sue encouraged me to do… 1. Sue and Weston, 2. Dorothy, 3. Feeling good, 4. New job, 5. God's hope, and future for me. I just feel a new excitement for my future. I can't wait to share this with Ruth, and my sis! I think about Dorothy's words, and I make the decision. I tell God I want a new place to work, with people who create, and encourage each other. I think about Sue's words, and I think about how she used the same analogy as my Grandma about apple's. I ponder it, and I hear the voice of truth say, *you do not leave the bad apple to spoil the others. Just don't let it be your focus. Toss it and move on.* I can go to sleep with that.

Another day at the office, Carla calls and lets me know that the perm is in if I want to stop by and get it, or she could bring it by. I tell her I'm going to go out and grab lunch, so I could swing by there quickly and grab it. "Ok, great! I'll see you around lunchtime." I think about what Evan told me, "she needs to bring it back to us." I think to myself, *I just won't say anything to him about it.*

I finish up with my two new customers. The first one was a guy, that Ben sent to me for a haircut, he was easy. But the next one, would not be that easy. This woman is what I think you call, "high maintenance," and I don't know that *anyone* would please her. It's funny, how people come in with pictures that are of people with 10 times the hair they have, and a whole different texture, and they want to look just like the picture. *Well I want to look like Farrah Fawcett too, but that ain't happening!* So what should've taken an hour, took nearly two hours. So if she comes back, I'm going to have to remember that! Double the time! Wish I could double the pay! I know everyone won't be easy to please, it sure does make me appreciate the ones that are!

It's lunch time, and I'm getting my purse to leave. Evan asks, "where are you going?" I answer him with, "lunch." "Did you ask?" "No, I just have a break, so I wanted to go get something to eat." "Well, I guess that's fine, but don't be gone long." "I won't."

I get in the car, and head for Don Juan's Mexican restaurant. I'm having a craving for some tacos. Soul food, is what this girl needs right now. I love tacos! I think that's probably one of my favorite foods. One of my new customer's, Shelly, works here. She told me that she would treat me to some tacos, telling me "they're the best in town!" I walk in and spot Shelly, she runs over to me and gives me a big hug! That's one thing I'm enjoying about this small town, it has a big happy family feel to it. I've had a few people say that they think it's clicky here, but I have not yet experienced that, and I'm glad.

Shelly sits me down and brings me some ice tea, and some chips with salsa. *Wow, this is some hot salsa, but it's delicious!* I laugh to myself because it makes me think of Wilma, keeping it spicy, oh what a visual! I haven't heard from her and it makes me wonder if she'll be back to me. I hope so. Here come my tacos! *Oh my, they are wonderful, Shelly's right! These are great tacos! I'll be back!* I finish up, and ask Shelly for my bill. She says to me, "oh no girl, this is on me, I told you I was treating you to the best tacos in town!" "Well you're right, they are the best tacos! I don't want you paying for me." As soon as I say it, I hear Dorothy's voice telling me, *sometimes the giver, sometime the receiver. Receive with gratitude.* So I say, "thank you so much for the special treat, Shelly!" "I'm glad to do it Hannah. I mean, look at how great I look 'cause of you girl!"

Well that makes me feel good. There's a feather in my cap today! It is a good feeling when you know you change somebody's attitude about themselves, sometimes it takes more than hair though. I think about Shelly, and I think *this is what we're supposed to do*. Encourage one another, and acknowledge what each of us is doing, to serve one another. To leave each other with the feeling of fulfillment, always. The good side of my list continues to grow.

I'm headed to Carla's shop. I'm excited to see her place, I've never been inside before. I pull into the parking lot, walk in, and there are two ladies under the dryer's. One is sitting in the chair getting her haircut. It's a lively place, it feels happy here! Carla says to me, "hey there, how are you today?" "I'm good, I just finished having the best tacos in town!" "Let me guess, you had lunch at Don Juan's." "Good guess! They are the best!" "Are you in a hurry?" "Kind of." "Ok, let me get the perm for you." She introduces me to Betty, who is getting her hair cut. "Nice to meet you!" "Nice to meet you as well, Hannah. I've heard good things about you!" "I'm glad for that!" "Sue is a good friend of mine, and has told me about you." "Oh I love Sue!" "I agree, she's pretty wonderful!" Out walks Carla with the perm, she hands it to me and thanks me. "You're welcome, I'm glad we had one for you."

"That is the nice thing about our town, everybody's pretty good about sharing. I know it hurts Evan sometimes to share, but he does it in spite of himself." We all laugh. "I'm glad you get that, Carla." "Oh I do. That's why I love to call and borrow from him. I like to think I'm helping him work on his holiness!" More laughter. Carla says to Betty, "I'm going to walk Hannah outside, I'll be right back." "Ok, nice meeting you again Betty," "you too, Hannah."

We walk out to my car, and Carla says to me, "Hannah, I want to ask you a question. I told you I was going to build onto my shop…" "Yes, I remember that." "Well, I don't want you to answer me right now, but I want you to think about maybe coming to work for me. I don't know your situation with Evan, but I would love to take time to sit with you, and discuss a business venture together." Wow. I tell her, "I would *love* to sit with you and discuss a business venture." "Well I know you got to run, as do I, so why don't you give me a call and let's plan a time to have lunch, or an evening drink or dinner." "What about Sunday? My week is kind of crazy, I started working part-time at the shoe store. So if we could meet on Sunday, that would be great for me!" "Sounds good, how about my sister's place for breakfast?" "I've never been there before, I always enjoy a new place to eat and I have a customer that works there, so it will be nice to see her. Meet for nine in the morning?" "Sure, see you then." "Okay then, it's a date."

Driving back to work, and I'm freaking out thinking, *oh my gosh, what does this mean? How do I look at Evan, knowing that I might be leaving him? Calm down Hannah, just breathe. You don't even know what's gonna happen yet so just take it one day at a time.* I'm excited and scared at the same time, it feels kind of good. Evan drives me crazy, but I still kind of feel guilty for feeling this good about leaving him! I'm thinking about the good feeling I had in Carla's shop. I like that feeling. "Listen to your spirit Hannah." I need to pray about this, and talk about it with my support team!

As soon as I get home I'm calling Ruth and my sis, and maybe my Dad. I just don't want to freak the ol'boy out! Well I might as well throw Mom, and Grandma in too.

Going into work, I'm feeling a little bit guilty. I don't know why. I think to myself, *why should I even care? He doesn't treat me like I matter anyhow, so I don't know that he would really care that I leave, except that he would not have me to bully.* How sad is that? Really Hannah, it's pretty pitiful, your work situation. It's like I'm in a bad marriage, or have this mean boyfriend that I never know how I'll be treated. Will he be nice to me? In a good mood, or a bad mood? Is he talking, or is he not talking? I always have a stomach ache thinking about work, and it is for one reason…the King!

I walk in to work, and *the King* has for me, a smart ass remark, as always. "So, where you go to lunch? To China? It took you long enough, didn't it?" "I was only gone for one hour." "Yeah well, you could've done it in only thirty minutes. I'm the boss around here, so don't get smart." "Well, I'm sorry I didn't realize you wanted me back in less than an hour." "Alright, you're back now so get to work! Towels need to be folded, and I want you to clean the bathroom. No sitting around." You got to be kidding me. He is pushing me out the door. I don't think I can run fast enough! Sitting around? I have never done that! Talk about working on your holiness!

Thank God this day is over! I think to myself, *I can't keep living like this, this is crazy*. Well I'm going to call Ruth, and the rest of the gang when I get home, and figure it all out. Everything in me, says *go, leave, run, fast!*

Oh, how it feels good to be home! I love my little home with Juanita and Jack! I laugh, thinking about something I once heard someone say, *there's two places you should have peace. In the grave, and in your home*. I do feel at peace here. My roomies aren't home yet. I sit down and stare out the window. *Ok God, show me the way*. I want to do what's right. I just didn't realize that being a grown-up was going to be this difficult. My vision so far, is not my reality. I better work on my vision!

I get the phone, and call Ruth to give her an earful. Phone rings and Ruth answers, "hey there my friend." "Oh hey, what's up?" "Well lots, I got a new job offer today!" "Wow, that's cool." "Yes, it is, except I have to tell Evan that I'm leaving him, and that makes me want to slit my wrist." "Oh Hannah, don't say that." "You're right, but I'm telling you, I have never encountered such a difficult person. I feel like I can get along with most people, but I just can't, for the life of me understand him." "You are one of the easiest people I know to get along with." "Yeah, but you're my best friend." "Yeah, so what's your point?" "Well, you're partial to me." "I am, I don't just hang out with anybody." "Well, I'm so glad we had this talk, so I know that I made your friend cut!" Laughter!

"So, when do you decide where you'll be working? Who is it, that gave you the offer?" "Her name is Carla, she is fun and very spunky! She borrowed a perm from us, and I went to pick it up and she followed me out to my car to gave me the offer. So I'm meeting her for breakfast on Sunday to discuss all the details." "It sounds good, you just have to go meet with her and see what she says." "I know, I just wish I did not have to do it. You know how I hate to disappoint people Ruth. Even a jerk like Evan!" "Oh Hannah, you're such a people pleaser!" "Don't go there Ruth, I know you hate that, but you're such a middle-child, and so am I!" More laughter! "Well one of my customers said that we are all a work in progress, so there is hope Ruth!" "Cool! I will tell my Mom to pray, you know she loves a mission." "I'm glad she does. Tell her to tell God, the girl needs a neon sign and someone to tell Evan for me." "You don't need a neon sign, I think you know what you're gonna do, you just go get the courage to do it!" "You're right, you know me so well Ruth!" "It's easy Hannah! By the way my mom is really missing you, she keeps asking when you're gonna come visit." "I know, I need to get home. I just don't have the money or time. That's another thing! I got a job at a shoe store, working two half-days a week, and on Monday's. So this girl does not have much down time." "I guess not. Sounds like you're going to be a workaholic, like your Dad." "Well there is worse things to be, and right now I have to do what I can. I just can't survive, on working at the beauty shop alone. So I will make lemonade out of my lemons, as my Mother would say."

"I guess I'll meet with her on Sunday, and make my decision. Tell Mama to keep me prayed up, and anybody else you want. It will take a big team of prayer warriors for this one. Ruth, I hope you can come visit me soon, there are so many people I want you to meet. My boss at the shoe store, is the coolest woman I've ever met! You will love her." "Ok, now I'm hurt. I thought I was the coolest woman you've ever met." Laughter! "Hopefully soon, I can get up there." "So, how is beauty school going by the way?" "Oh, I wish you had not asked me that question." "Why, what's going on?" "Well I quit." "Oh no, you're Pinky from *Grease*, a beauty school dropout!" I start laughing, "I'm sorry Ruth! You got to admit it's kind of funny." "Well, tell my Mom and Dad that." "But, it is pretty funny. We do think alike, you and I." "I thought the very same thing, as I walked out of beauty school with all my stuff. I could hear Frankie Valli, singing *beauty school dropout* to me." I start laughing so hard, I can't stop. "I will get a lot of mileage out of this story, thank you Ruth!" "Oh great, I'm glad I could take your mind off things, I guess there are far much worse things you could be, than a beauty school dropout." "I'm sorry Ruth, what happened?" "I just don't have a passion for it." "You love hair and makeup!" "I know, I do for me, but I don't want to do the shampoo sets! I don't know Hannah." "Well, you will figure it out Ruth, don't freak out." "Me, freak out? Never!" "Life is funny. Right,

I've got to get going. I miss you so much my friend, I hope we can see each other soon!" "Me too! Love you!" "Love you! Mizpah!" "Mizpah!"

What would I do without Ruth? She brings such good to my life, and not to mention fun! I feel bad for her, she will get a lot of flack from her parents for this. I will pray they don't give her too much. I really can't believe that she quit, she is more into beauty than I am. I do feel her, because I felt that way at first in beauty school. We have an idea of what we think it will be, and I'm learning quickly, it is not always what we had envisioned. As I think about it, I realize it is not just about hair, nails and makeup. Something happens when you are touching people, and giving them a service. *Woah, Hannah! That sounds like you're a hooker!* Making myself laugh! Well really, there is a connection made between you and the customer, that becomes deeper and deeper each time you meet. I'm starting to realize the beauty shop is not just about how we look on the outside, it is how we feel on the inside. You can make someone look amazing, but if they don't feel that on the inside, your job as a hairdresser just changed to psychologist and motivational speaker! So maybe all that is too much for my Ruth at this time. I will share that with her next time we talk.

What a week it's been, it's Friday and I have a date with Ben tonight. I'm excited and I'm nervous! What to wear? I model several things for Juanita and Jack, and they finally help me settle on a skirt and blouse, with my boots. Of course, Juanita will decorate me with her jewellery to finish my look. I feel pretty! So glad, I'm liking the reflection in the mirror. Not always the case.

Sweet Jack, tells me he wants to take me dancing when he's big! Oh, the boy melts my heart! I hope I have a son or two like him one day. Here goes my thoughts, *could Ben be my son's father?* Oh Hannah! I'm just going dancing, but Wilma is praying for me. We shall see?

Hope the day goes fast. I get to work and Evan and Carrie are outside, sitting on the bench and it looks serious. Oh I don't need this today! God keep me in your bubble, don't let Evan ruin my day. I hear the voice of truth say, *Hannah you're always in my bubble, and he can only ruin your day if you allow him to.* Ok I will keep my focus on the good today! I begin to sing to myself, I have a date with Ben! I walk in and say good morning. Carrie says it back, while Evan tells me he needs me to cover for him today. So now I will have to work until six-thirty. Oh no, I have a date at seven! Really, I am struggling with my focus. This is where I need my Mother's balls! She has always said says she has more than any man!

So here it goes, "Evan I have somewhere to be at seven tonight. I can't possibly get out of work at six-thirty, and be ready by seven." He replies, "well it looks like you'll have to change your plans." "I can't change my plans, and I've had these plans for over a week now." Carrie seems to be very uncomfortable, we all do actually. Not Evan, he's comfortable with being a jerk! I'm standing my ground, "I'm sorry Evan, but I can't! I will help you to try and change people around, but I cannot stay that late tonight." "I don't think you understand Hannah, I wasn't asking you if you could, I'm telling you that you will! You're the one that needs to change things around girl!" His face is actually turning red, and he looks like he's on fire! Something happens to me, I just want to laugh. I remain calm, and tell him, "you know Evan, I have done a great job for you, and never ever do you say *thank you*. I'm sorry, but you're not gonna do this to me today, I will not allow you to treat me like I'm nothing. My plans are as important as your plans and I'm sorry that I can't do it for you today. I would if I didn't have plans, but this is important to me. So you need to change your plans. One more thing Evan, you should try some gratitude. I can't believe the wonderful people that you're around, and you still continue to be such a mean, angry person! I have tried to be positive and find the good in things, and you make it such a struggle every single day. And I'm just tired of it, I'm tired of you being mean and putting me down, and making me feel like I'm nothing. You're wrong, I am something, and I'm something wonderful. And I'm sorry that you missed it."

Oh my goodness, I feel like Mohammed Ali right now. I just knocked him out! Evan is speechless, I can't believe it. He is fire red, with his mouth wide open, and for once nothing's coming out of it! Poor Carrie, she's white as a ghost! And I just want to do a victory dance! Ok, now it hits me what I just did! Evan finally gets words, and says to me, "okay then Hannah, have it your way. You can give me two weeks and be gone." I drop another ball, and out it comes. "No Evan, it's always your way and that's the problem with you. That's why you probably, will never have anybody that can work very long with you, because it's your way or the highway. There is no other way, but Evan's way! I'm an idiot for even trying to stay here this long. So I gladly give you my two weeks." Evan is in shock, he cannot believe that little, pitiful Hannah who would let him just run her over, tell her she was no good, and slap her ass daily, is in his face! I can't believe how good this feels! "I'm sorry Carrie, I hate that this had to happen in front of you right now. Carrie, in her sweet little soft voice then says, "I'm sorry, and hope you all can work things out." I think, *really Carrie?* I think we just did work things out. Ouch! “I’m going, and I have a customer coming soon I need to get ready. I’m sorry this had to happen but, it did.” “Are you leaving for the day still?” “Don’t worry about it Hannah, now I know how you really are.” Oh Evan, you have no idea who I really am! I hate when people like you, treat people badly and when they stand up for themselves, you try to turn it around and make them look like they’re the mean jerk! Well you’re not going to do that to me! I’m done trying with you. Proverbs in the *Bible* say, *don’t hang out with angry people lest you become like them.* I’ll take God’s advice. So thanks for the lesson Evan, I shall remember them always! You were a good teacher!

Finally the day’s done, it’s five o’clock and I’m headed home. Wait until Juanita hears about this day! I’m home, my place of peace! I tell Juanita about the day, in a nutshell. I don’t have time to go into it all, I’ve got to get dressed for my date. She tells me, she’s proud of me for standing up for myself, and not to feel bad, then gives me a hug and says, “you know Hannah, you just grew up a whole bunch, girl.”

It’s seven o’clock, Ben pulls in the driveway. I’m off to the ball! He asks about my day. I say, “oh man, that’s a loaded question. I gave my two weeks notice.” “Okay, wow, you did have quite a day! I guess dancing will be good for you tonight, we’ll lighten it up and have some fun, how about that?” “Sounds good to me!” I really like Ben, I hope he’s liking me too! We get to the Blue Moon, and in we go for a night of fun. I get in, without being carded! Yippy! Ben and I meet his friends, and we all have a great time! Ben and I dance the night away! I am loving my life! Amazing what a cute guy, and some dancing can do for a girl!

CHAPTER 5

What School Doesn't Teach You

I wake up early this morning, after my amazing date with Ben. I didn't get in until two in the morning, I can't believe I'm already awake at 6:30 a.m. Laying in bed, I'm thinking about yesterday and going over it in my mind. Thinking I should feel afraid and scared, but I don't, I just feel excited. I can't believe this is me, usually I would be freaking out! But I just feel such a peace about my future. I guess Juanita is right, maybe I did grow up some this week! Well, it's like I always say, *you can let life make you better or bitter*, I'm choosing better!

Guess I better get up, and face the day. I do have to be in at work for 9:00 a.m. Thank goodness, Evan is not there today, but I have two weeks left with him. I'm looking forward to tomorrow morning, and having breakfast with Carla. It will be refreshing to be with a positive, uplifting person.

Thinking back to Ruth, I'm realizing more and more that there's so much that school can't teach us. I get up, and start making coffee, Juanita walks in, "hey what are you doing up so early? You didn't get in until late." "I know, I just couldn't sleep." "So how was it?" "It was a wow! Ben is a really nice guy, and all of his friends were great too! His brother's girlfriend and I really hit it off! She works at the bank. Her name is Nicole Hixon, do you know her?" "I think I know who she is, just from seeing her at the bank."

"Well that's cool, I'm glad you had a great time, how are you feeling about work?" "Well today is gonna be fine, because Evan's not there, but I'd be lying if I didn't say that I was a little nervous about the next two weeks. It won't be fun, but I'm gonna stay strong and do the right thing." "Well I'm sorry that my cousin chose to be such a jerk to you, but I see you will be better off, and you have learned to find your voice and power! Sometimes we need the ruff sand paper people in our lives for that very reason!" I laugh! "I have never heard that analogy before, I like it. I can't thank you enough for your friendship and your understanding, and I feel so blessed to get to be here, and live with you and Jack." "I feel the same about you." "I miss our little Jack when he's away at his Dad's." "Yeah, it always feels kind of strange not to have him, I'm so used to him being here, but it's good for him, and for me!" "Yes I know it is." "What plans do you have for the weekend?" "You're not the only one that got a date. I've got a date tonight, he's a musician. Super nice guy, really cute too! We'll see." "It's funny how we always think about the cuteness of someone, my Dad always tells me, that we would pick better mates if we all were blind and we went with our hearts, instead of our eyes. I don't know, maybe he's right, but I *do* have eyes and I *do* like cute!" "Well your Dad is a wise man. I'm sure he's right, but you have a point, we do have eyes, so cute matters!" We laugh!

"I better get my cuteness to the shower, and get ready for work." "Hey, I still owe you a night out. We never did go, you got sick and it didn't work out, so we need to plan that for sure." "Yes, I would love a night out with you!"

Alright, I've got my cuteness on! Off to work I go, *hi ho, hi ho!* My first customer's Polly and Rosie, are two older sisters, sent to me from Carla. She could not fit them into her schedule, so she sent them over to me. They will be weekly clients, so that will be nice to know I have that income every week! That's another thing school can't teach, the tenacity it takes to be in this business. Walk into work, and it's so peaceful when Evan is not in this place. I get ready for Rosie and Polly, I can't wait to meet them. I see them walking up the sidewalk, they look like two, sweet little ladies. I hope that's the truth. Door opens and I say, "good morning I'm Hannah." At the same time, they both say, "good morning Hannah, it's a pleasure to meet you." "You too," I say. "Come on in, who is going to go first this morning?" "I will," says Polly. "Well then, Rosie make yourself at home, and you come with me Polly, I will get you shampooed." I can tell that I'm going to love these two. They have the best southern accents! I find out, they are from Mississippi. I ask, "how in the world did you get here?" "Well Polly was a nurse in the Army, and is retired." She tells me she lost her one true love in World War ll. "Oh, how sad." "Yes it was," she replies. "But here's the thing, some people never have that kind of love in their whole lives, and I just feel fortunate to have had it with *my Pete*. He is the best man I've ever known, besides my daddy, and I feel fortunate to have been loved by such a grand man! I just wished I had more time with him, that's all, but I'll see him again in heaven, I know that to be true." "Wow Polly, that's quite the love story! It's pretty wonderful to have that strong of a love, that you can never find anything to replace it." "Well I think so. Anyhow, back to your question on how I found my way to Tall Pines. My sister Rosie, and her family moved here after her husband Jerry got out of the army. They would visit here to get out of the heat of Texas, where they lived at the time, and determined they would move here as soon as he got out. They bought the dry cleaner's here and have been here for 12 years now. When I decided to retire, they invited me to live here with them, knowing I have no children of my own to help care for me in my old age. Their girls have been as close as I could come, to having my own! They are all so good to me! I'm so blessed!" "I can see the bond that you and Rosie have, just watching you walk up the sidewalk together. I have that with my sis too!" "Well I'd say we are two lucky girls to have such wonderful sisters!" "So true, I don't know what I would do without my sis! I always say, *she is my calm in the storms of life!*" "That's a good one Hannah! I like that, and I agree, that is what a sister should be!" "Well let's get you under the dryer." "Ok, I'm ready for a nap, the dryer always puts me to sleep!"

"Rosie, you're up! Come on back, and we'll get you shampooed." "Ok, I'm ready, my hair is just filthy dirty! I can't tell you how grateful I am to you for taking us in, we have been looking for a new hairdresser, ours just up and left town." "Really? Who was it?" "Her name was Gwen, she's been doing our hair for five years, but decided she needed to move to the city. Not enough action here for her. She was nice enough, but I never really felt a real connection to her. You know what I mean?" "Yeah I do!" "I already feel more of a connection with you, Hannah!" "Wow! Thank you! I feel the same way about you too!" Finished shampooing Rosie, and she remarks, "and that, is the best shampoo I've had in years! Thank you Hannah!" "I'm glad you liked it!" "I always say, that is the best part of getting my hair done, and if I was rich, I would have someone to shampoo my hair everyday! Just not the same when you do it yourself!" "That is the truth!" "I'm glad I get to have it done once a week by you!" "Glad I can do it for you!" So as I'm rolling Rosie's hair, she tells me about her husband Jerry, and her two daughters, Annie and Sally. "They have worked together running their business all these years, and have been very close. Well, until now that is." "What do you mean?" I ask. "My eldest daughter just married, and has married into a family with money." "Well that does not sound so bad." "It should not be, but she is now treating us like we are not quite good enough, and we embarrass her. It makes me so sad! I have not said a lot to Polly about it, because I don't want to make her feel bad or in the middle of things. She adores my girls and I would not want that to change." " Well I just hate that for you, but hopefully she'll get grounded again. She'll come back to her senses, and realize what a blessing it is to have a family who loves, and supports each other like yours does." "Well thank you Hannah!" "I know I have just met you, but I can see the kind of love and respect that you and your sister have for each other. So I know that has been given and passed to your daughters." "That is so kind of you to say!" "I mean it." "I know you do!" "Please know I won't share this conversation with Polly." "I would be grateful if you would not." "How about we pinky-swear?" "Okay! I just love you already, Hannah!" "Well aren't I blessed!" "I am going to call Carla, and tell her I could just kiss her for sending us to you! I was so upset about not getting in with her, but God put us is the perfect place, with you!" "That makes me happy to hear! I do have to tell you that I need your confidence now, I have put in my two weeks notice here, and I'm meeting with Carla in the morning for breakfast and hopefully going to work for her. So I will keep you posted." "Well we will go wherever you are, dear." "I'm grateful!" "I will keep your news to myself for now." "That would be great. Ok then miss Rosie, let's get you under the dryer, looks like sister is in dreamland. Funny how the dryer puts you to sleep, they do have that effect on everyone. I love to sit under one, especially in the winter." "Yes, they can get a little hot in the summer!" "True!" I have a moment to sit, until Polly's dryer goes off. What a great morning! I think about all that Dorothy said to me, and how when I make a decision and share it with God, He is working it all out, good for me! So many times I would read my *Bible*, and think to myself *how in the world does this work in my life?* He is showing me *how*, day by day! I think about how funny life is, and how religion has always somehow confused me at times, but in the deepest part of me I've always known, that God was for *me* and that he loved *me*. Although, there was a time as a little girl that I thought God was mean! I realized that was religion, not God! God's love, and God, is good! I love you God, thank you for answering my prayer! You're awesome!

I hear the dryer click off, Polly's ready and she looks drowsy, but comes out of it. "Are you awake?" "Well I'm trying to get there," she says. I get her combed out, and she is fixed up for a week. I don't know how they stand it for a week, but I'm from the new age of washing your hair daily. She tells me how grateful she is to me, and that she loves how I did her hair. Oh that's a relief! I still don't feel like I'm the best at shampoo sets, because I like the blow dry and curling iron look myself. I'm told by many a lady, they just don't stay in! It's Rosie's turn now. I get her fixed up for the week, and scheduled for next week. I'm so happy I get to see them every week! She loves her hair too! More good news! Rosie tells me that she is calling Carla to tell her how wonderful the experience was with me, she winks at me and says, "that won't hurt your job interview!" "No it won't," I reply. "See you girls next week!" "Thanks again!" My day flew by! My late night has caught up to me. I'm ready to go home and put my feet up.

• • •

This is the best, laying here listening to my favorite music. The one thing that would make it better is, Ben here laying next to me! The phone rings, and my heart starts pounding with excitement that it will be Ben! I jump up and answer, "hello, is Hannah there?" "This is Hannah." "Hey there, it's Ben." "I'm glad you called, was just thinking about you, and what a great time I had last night! You have a great bunch of friends!" "Thanks, I think so too! Well Josh tends to be an over-achiever when it comes to drinking." That's Ben's brother. "That's a fun way to put it!" "Makes it sound more positive, right?" "Right! Oh well, we can all have our moments. He was funny and I really like his girlfriend!" "Yeah Nicole is great, she is like a sister to me." "I can see that." "She really liked you too!" "Oh I'm glad." "So what are you up to tonight?" "I'm just laying here listening to Fleetwood Mac, relaxing." "Sounds good." "Would you like to join me?" "I think I would! Is it good with your roommate? I know she has a young son." "She is out on a date, and Jack is with his Dad for the weekend, so we are good to go. Thanks for asking." See? *Just another thing to love about Ben!* "Ok then, I will be over in a hour or so. How about I stop and grab us a pizza? I haven't eaten yet, how about you?" "No, I haven't either, so that would be good." "Any preference?" "Not really, except no anchovies." "No worries there!" "Ok I'll see you soon!" "Ok, see ya!" *Woohoo, Ben's coming over!* I begin to dance around the house. I have not had these feelings for a guy before! I feel so comfortable with him. It's kind of scary! Oh well, I am going for it! It feels too good to be true, I guess that is what is scaring me. That's also kind of sad, that we feel something so good and think, this can't be right. Oh my gosh, I don't want to go there! *Hannah, enjoy the good!* Ok, what to wear? Because the boy has eyes and I want to be pleasing to them, time to get my cuteness on! I better set the mood and light some candles. We had just one kiss last night, and it was amazing! So I am excited to kiss him again! I hope Wilma is working in the morning when I have breakfast with Carla, so I can tell her that her prayer is working! I think I found Mr. Right! It can't be wrong if it feels this right. *Oh Hannah!!* I see Bens truck pulling into the drive way. Oh, be still my heart! He has the best smile, and I do love his dimples. I open the door, and he gives me the sweetest kiss. Oh Lord, I think I'm in love! Crazy! No *hello*, just straight action! My Dad has always said, *you know a man by their actions not their words*. Well I'm liking his actions. Who needs pizza? I will have Ben! I would love to try living on love! "I like that, we are off to a good start." "Yeah, I've been thinking about kissing you all day. So sorry, I could not stop myself." "No apologies needed, I was thinking the same thing. Come in the kitchen and set the pizza down." I get out two plates and grab some napkins. He comes up behind me and grabs me around the waist. I take a deep breath! Turn around and our lips connect and we can't stop. Oh, I'm in heaven. I think I could kiss this man forever! I feel panic set in. Why do we go to the *what if* place? I pull back and say, "do you want a pizza break?" He laughs and says sure. So I flip the album, and we sit down on the couch with our pizza and take a couple of bites before we are making out again, like we are magnets and can't keep away from each other. We truly can't stop! Ben says to me, "you are addictive Hannah!" "Back at ya Ben," I say. We laugh, and try to stop ourselves again and eat.

It's 12:30 a.m. and Ben feels like he needs to leave, everything in me wants him to stay, but he's right he needs to leave. I'm not ready for that next step with him. Even though everything in my flesh is saying yes, my mind and my heart are saying *no not yet Hannah*. I'll tell you what, the flesh is a hard one to battle! Another thing to love about Ben? He really is such a kind considerate caring man. So we pry ourselves away from each other and I tell him we have to say goodbye from across the room, "because if I get near you, you're a magnet for my lips!" He laughs, we both do. "Well you're one for mine, so you're right we need to keep our distance! Can I call you tomorrow? Maybe we could take a hike or a picnic." "That sounds fun! I do have my meeting with Carla at 9 a.m., and I'm not sure how long it will last. I'll be free after that though, so how about I call you after that." "Ok then, I'll wait to hear from you. Sweet dreams!" "Oh I will," I answer back. "You too!" "They will be of you Hannah!" "Go, because that just makes we want to kiss you more!" "Wow I'm good!" We laugh. "Yeah, you are! Night Ben!" He smiles and walks out. *Oh my heart!* I get ready for bed and all I can think about is the wonderful, of Ben. I think about Polly's love for Pete, and how she called him a *grand man*. I get it, that's how I feel about Ben. I would say he is a grand man! What did I do, to deserve this amazing man. Here comes the thoughts, *maybe he is just a good actor, you don't know that much about him Hannah.* I say shut up to those thoughts, and trust my instincts. I will give him the chance that he deserves. So far, it's pretty wonderful! I'm staying on the ride! I lay my head on my pillow, and fall asleep on my Ben cloud!

Wake up to the sound of cock-a-doodle-doo, cock-a-doodle-doo. Time to wake up Hannah. Oh my, what a great night sleep I had! I'm excited for this day, I can't wait to meet Carla this morning and hear what she has to say, and hopefully go to work for her. I cannot wait to see Ben again this afternoon! I walk out to the kitchen to get some coffee and I notice Juanita has not come home, so I'm thinking that her and Mick hit it off. I don't know because I haven't heard from her. Funny I feel kind of motherly, I'm thinking *is she okay?* I wish she would have called me and said she wasn't coming home. Hopefully she'll call this morning or show up soon. I just don't like not knowing. I'm sure everything is okay, but there's just always those weird stories you hear about. I start to go there in my mind, but I'm not going to. I'm sure she had a great time, and all is well. She's a grown woman so I need to keep that in mind, I know when you love people, you want to protect them and I do love her. I think I'm going to go for a coffee and just wait for Carla at *My Sister's Place. I'm a big girl now, I drink coffee!* I smile at that thought. I think I'll get ready and get there early and see if Wilma is working and tell her about her answer to my prayer, Ben. I don't want her to feel funny, because I have not heard from her about her hair. This is the weird part about this business. I want to please everyone, but I know I won't. I still want to be friends, even if I don't do their hair. I guess it's hard to not take it personally at times, and I need not to. Also, there are the people you will never please! I continue to be a work in progress, thank God he won't give up on me! Now that's good news!

• • •

I'm dressed and ready to head out the door. As I do, the phone rings. I hope it's Juanita. "Hello?" "Hey there, are you worried?" "Kinda, but I decided to try not to. Did you have fun?" "Yes it was great! You should have come out." "Well I was going to, and Ben called, so sorry I chose to make out with him!" "Ok, can't blame you." "So did you do some making out to?" "I sure did! We'll talk later, I just wanted to call so you would not worry about me. I know you have your meeting this morning, so wanted to wish you luck!" "You're the best! Thank you for calling me. When you coming home?" "Mick is cooking me breakfast, so after that. What are you doing after your meeting?" "Ben wants to have a picnic or hike." "Ok, you two are on now, three days in a row?" "I know, right? He is amazing!" "Ok, we will talk later. I'm going to meet my ex and get Jack at four." "Ok, I will see you before that I'm sure." "See ya, bye!"

That's a relief to know she's safe and okay. And wow, she spent the night with Mick? That seems a little quick to me, but who am I to judge. *Just run my own race.* Besides, Juanita is ten years older than me. I guess, maybe it's different after you've been married. I'm just a little weird I guess, my religious upbringing makes you feel like you're some kind of whore if you even think about sex! To be a virgin, or not to be a virgin? It's like your used goods, and not worth much if you're not. I don't agree with that, I think that we will make choices that are not always the best, but we should not be put down for those decisions. There is no such thing as perfect, and as I think of all the people God used, I can't think of one perfect except for Jesus! They all had their issues just like me and the rest of man kind. As I ponder this, I see that the one thing they had in common was that they all had a heart for God! More good news, He can use me! I do have a heart for Him!

I pull into *My Sister's Place*, and get a parking spot right in the front. My mother always told me, go to the front and I'll be darned if there's not always a parking space available, so I think *I'll start doing that!* She would say, *no one ever thinks they'll be a parking place in the front, so they just settle and park way back.* Well she's not a settler, I'll tell you that. *Believe, receive!* I often think it's God's way of just delighting us, and showing us that he does care about every little thing that we care about, so if front row parking is important I believe that he wants us to have that! Some people would say that's crazy, so call me crazy! I believe! I walk in, and there's Wilma. She runs over to me, "well, how you been girl? I've been thinking about you, look at this hair, I'm a mess! I just have not taken the time to get it done, and I'll tell you, I had to cut it some myself the other night. It's just horrible, so when can I get into you?" "Soon I hope!" "Well I have time on Tuesday, could you do that?" "They'll be putting the schedule up anytime now, so I'll look at it and see, hopefully they'll get it up before you leave. If not, you can call me at home or call me on Tuesday morning." "How many you got coming, sugar? "Just two of us." "Okay, follow me right over here. I've got the perfect window seat for you!" "Well I've been excited to talk to you Wilma! I was hoping you would be here today!" "Really, what about?"

"Your prayer for me." "Oh I've told God about your mountain. So tell me now, what he has done." "Oh he moved it alright!"

"I have met the most wonderful man and I'm so excited, a little scared, but I'm really excited! It happened the next day after I had done your hair." "I told you honey, when I pray you watch out, because Mountain's move, I believe!" " Well you made me believe! It moved fast!" "I'm so happy for you Hannah, I just want everyone to have what I have with Charlie! Nothing better than a good partner! I can't wait to hear all about it when you do my hair." "I can't wait to tell you!" "Who ya meeting?" "Carla, from *The Hair Tamer.*" "She's a great gal! Hard to get into see, she's busy!" "That's what I hear. Well I might go to work for her, long story." "Well, maybe God moved more than one mountain for you." "You're right Wilma! Thank you for praying for me!" "Oh listen girl, it's my joy! I just love seeing what God does!" "Me too!" "Got to get back to work, look over the menu and I'll be back with coffee. You do want some, don't you?" "Oh yes I do! Cream too please." "You got it!"

In walks Carla, oh my she has a different color of hair again! This is funny. Making her way to our table, she talks to almost everyone! She is well-known I see, and appears to be liked by many. Good sign! "Hey Hannah! How are you?" "Well Carla, I'm really great, except for my job." "What's going on?" So I give her the story. "Well," she replies. "You've lasted longer than most!" "I don't know if that's good or bad." "I think good and bad. Good, because you tried to do right and hoped Evan would get better. And bad, because it was such a stressful work place." "I just have never encountered such a negative, angry person!" "Well I wish you could work with me right away, but we're still under construction. Good news is, it should be done in time for you to start in two weeks. That is if you want to work with me?" "Yes, yes, yes, a million times! I do have to work at the shoe store two half-days, and on Monday's all day. Will that be okay with you?" "It's fine with me." "I just needed extra money, I did not realize how hard it is to get established." "Well I hear good things about you Hannah, so it won't be long 'til you are really making it doing hair." "I hope so but I'm looking forward to my time with Dorothy. She is amazing!" "Well I don't see a problem with you working at the shoe store. I can't believe Evan didn't have a problem with it." "Well Dorothy is the one who worked that out for me." "Oh, smart!" "That she is." "We need to discuss the money thing. What do you want to do, booth rent? Or would you rather do a percentage. Here's what I think, why not try percentage for awhile, until you get established and then we can do a booth rent later." "That sounds perfect, Carla. What is the percentage?" "I do sixty-percent to you and forty-percent to the shop. I pay all supplies and bills." "Great! This is an answer to a prayer for me!" "It is for me too!"

"I'm glad it's working out perfectly. I did feel like I need to do my two weeks' at Evan's because I think it's the right thing. That's what I would want someone to do for me even if he's not doing the right thing. I really would rather not see him another day, but I'm going to suck it up and do it!" "Well here's the good news Hannah, time goes fast and two weeks will be done before you know it!" "That's true." "So let's order and eat." Wilma comes over and takes our order. We decide on huevos rancheros, they sound yummy! And they did not disappoint, they were delicious! It was a great morning. Carla and I walk out to our cars, she hugs me and tells me she's really excited about our future together. "I thinks it's gonna be great!" "No," she says, "I know it's gonna be great!" I just feel so refreshed after spending the morning with her, she's just such a breath of fresh air! Of course, even Frankenstein could be a breath of fresh air after dealing with Evan! I laughed to myself, but really she is a great person to be around.

I head for home, pull in the driveway and Juanita's car is there. I'm going to get the scoop from her and call Ben. I walk in and holler. "Hello!" Juanita walks out of her room and answers back, "hello! Well you are glowing," she says to me. "You have a glow yourself!" We laugh! "So how was it?" I ask. "Felt weird at first, because it's been 10 years since I have kissed anyone but James, Jack's Dad." "Yeah, I bet that was a little weird !" "I really like Mick though. We'll see how it goes. That's all we can do right?"

"So tell me about your night." "Oh my gosh I just can't believe he's so perfect, it's almost too scary to think that it could be for real. He's just such a gentleman, I just can't get over how considerate, kind and thoughtful he is. I know this is gonna sound corny but I'm telling you, I could kiss that man forever. It's like he's a magnet, I see him and I just want to put my lips on his lips! It's crazy." "Well it sounds good to me!" "I know, I'm staying on the ride. I'm not getting off, but I just get scared that maybe it's not everything I think it's gonna be. Oh well, like you said we'll see." "Hannah, it's never gonna be perfect." "I'm not expecting perfect I don't think, it's just that he feels perfect right now, it's crazy to me that I can't find anything wrong with the guy! We'll see?" "Yeah, you will have to give time to this one Hannah. We are not perfect and you will start to find flaws, I'm pretty sure he's flawed somehow. We all are." "Oh don't I know." "I don't want to be negative, I'm just telling you there will be flaws. That doesn't mean that it's still not the right one, you just gotta find the one who's flaws you can live with, that's what I've determined." "That's pretty good advice Juanita, I will think about that. So will you see Mick again soon?" "Yes, actually we are going on motorcycle ride in an hour. I think he likes me!" "What's not to like!" I say. "Oh your a good friend Hannah." "I try!" "I told him I can't see him when I have Jack right now. I just can't do that to him now. I mean, he is just now getting use to his life and I don't want to mess that up. Plus if I introduce a new man into his life it will only be because I'm in love. So not there yet. Mick was great about it though. He has a busy life, with his day job and his music." "Well it's a good sign that he understands about Jack." "I agree. I need to finish getting ready." "I need to call Ben." Juanita laughs. I ask, "what?" She says, "you light up just saying his name. Could it be love? What do we say?" "We'll see."

I pick up the phone and call Ben, no answer? Oh I hate this, I immediately feel sad. *Stop it Hannah!* I will try back in ten minutes. I get my laundry together, and ask Juanita if she needs any done. She hands me a few things and goes to Jack's room and gets a few things of his. "Thanks," she says. "No worries," I say. "Ben didn't answer the phone, so I'm killing time and I do need to get it done. I start my shoe store job this week." "Oh yeah, I almost forgot." "I'm excited about it! Oh, and you look great!" "Not feeling it, but thanks!" I don't know what it is with us girls, why we feel pretty one day and not the next? I don't ever remember my brothers doing that. I wonder if mirrors are where the problem began, or has it just always been this way? Here I go, somebody stop me! I hear a motorcycle pull up. Must be Mick. He's pretty cute! He comes up to the door and knocks, I open it. "You must be Mick." "Well yes I am, good guess!" "I'm Hannah, Juanita is finishing getting dressed." He comes in and I say, "have a seat, can I get you something to drink? Some water? I'm not sure what we have, but I know we have water." "No I'm good thanks." "Well she should be out any minute." Out walks Juanita. Mick says, "wow I didn't think you could look prettier than you did last night, but you do!" "That's what I told her!" "Ok if two are saying it, it must be true." "Well have fun and be safe!" I'm acting like such a mother today! They get on the Harley, and off they ride. I'm happy for her, she needed this. I don't know if he will be her Prince Charming, but he is giving her new hope! We all need hope to carry us forward and it comes in different forms.

I picked up the phone to call Ben again. Oh God, please let him answer. It rings a couple of times, and he picks up. "Hello?" "Hey it's Hannah." "Oh good, I had to step out for a little bit. I had a work issue so I had to go load some stuff for tomorrow. So I was hoping I didn't miss your call." "I did try to call you and didn't get you, so I figured you had to do something or for some reason you were away from the phone. So I'm calling you back!" "I'm glad you did. So do you still feel like a picnic or hike?" "I just want to be with you Hannah, I want to do whatever you want. "Good answer Ben!" "Am I winning?" "YES!" "I like that!" "I think we are both winning!" "You're right Hannah, we are! I have a great little spot I love to go to, and I would love to share it with you. We do have to hike a little ways, but not too far. It takes about twenty minutes." "Ok, how about I make some sandwiches and we picnic too?" "Sounds like a good time to me. Think we will eat?" "Oh you're funny Ben!" "We can if we want, or not. So what do like on your sandwich?" "Mayo, and mustard." "Ok, come get me." "I'm there in fifteen or less!" "I hope less!" "See ya!"

I finish making the sandwiches just as Ben pulls up. He knocks, and I open the door. "Perfect timing!" "Yes!" he says. And we are lip locked again! "Hannah I'm sorry, I just can't stop myself from kissing you!" "Don't apologize please! The feeling is mutual." "I just don't want to scare you." "You don't scare me. Well that's not totally true. What do you mean by that?" "Well I don't want to scare you either. I just really, really like you. And I guess that's scary."

"Let's just enjoy the day and forget about being scared. Deal?" "Okay deal." We shake hands, get our picnic, load up in the truck and off we go for an adventure. We pull up to this beautiful lake. "Wow this is breathtaking I've never been here." "Yeah, it's one of my favorite spots," he says. "I feel honored that you brought me here, I love it already!" "Just wait 'til we hike back to my special spot, you'll really say wow!" So Ben puts our picnic in his backpack, and off we go. It's an uphill climb in the beginning, and then we drop off and walk along the river's edge. I am just taking in the beauty that surrounds me, and I feel blessed once again to live in this amazing place. "Ben, do you ever think about leaving here?" He says, "no, not really you know. I have to leave here quite a bit for work and I'm away for a month or two at a time, and so I'm always grateful to return." That kind of takes me back for a minute. I didn't realize that he would be gone a month or two at a time, but I'm not going to let that bother me right now. I'm choosing to stay in the moment and just enjoy! Then he asks, "what about you?" "Well not really, I love it here and love the people too. You never know I guess." "Yeah, I guess we never know for sure. Life can throw ya a curve ball every now and then." "That's for sure! Like my boss!" We laugh. "I'm glad that is all working out for you Hannah." "Me too! I hope these two weeks go fast." "I hope so, for a couple of reasons." "Oh really, how so?" "Well I'm leaving tomorrow, and will be gone for a couple of weeks. I have a big job in Clovis, and it requires me to be there." Ok that was quick, a curve ball already? I feel a sadness and think to myself, this is not good. Or is it?

We get to his special spot, and my goodness the rocks are huge, and there's a big swimming hole with waterfalls everywhere. The trees seem to touch the sky! I'm looking up and Ben grabs me around the waist, and begins to kiss my neck. Oh this is heaven! At that moment my heart took a picture. I never want tomorrow to come! I ask God to make this day longer. He did it for Joshua in the *Bible*, so I know He can for me. I laugh to myself, I will share this with Wilma. She will be proud that I asked God to stop the sun! Ben and I lay our blanket down and we take off our shoes and step into the river. Yikes this is cold! It's really slippery walking, and my feet are sensitive so there is a lot of weird noises coming out of me. Ben laughs at me, and then down he goes in the water! Who is laughing now! I give him my hand, and down I go! Oh man, this is the coldest water I have ever felt! We manage to get up and we are soaked! We are looking at each other and at the same time say to one another, "you are purple!" Ben pulls me to him and says, "I'll warm you up Hannah." I don't doubt that! We kiss and I feel like time has stopped for this moment. "Okay," Ben says. "Let's see about drying off." "I'm so glad this is a warm day!" "Sorry I got you wet Hannah." "I think you're not sorry." He starts laughing, "you're right, I loved getting you wet! I'm starting to see you have a side to you that is a little ornery." "Oh no, you are on to me." "Yes, I am! I hope you want to continue to figure me out." "I must say you have my curiosity, so I'm going to keep playing." We sit on the blanket and I pull out our sandwiches. We are both hungry so we make a deal, no touching until we finish eating.

Ben and I are laughing at each other. "We're like a game show, *Let's Make a Deal*, everything is a deal with us. Life's a deal, it's just one big deal. You're constantly making deals," Ben says. "I never thought of it that way I guess you're right, we are always making deals somehow or another. I love making deals with you Ben!" "I feel the same way about you Hannah! I would like to make a deal with you right now, can I kiss you?" "Yes, but." "But what?" Ben says. "But, I get to say when you stop." "Well I guess I'll take your deal. This is my favorite deal yet!" Ben smiles at me and puts that smile of his on my lips. We are side by side and Ben rolls on top of me, and oh I hear the voices of past yelling, *don't you let him that close!* They only want one thing! At one point in my life, my Mother had me so scared I thought I could get pregnant just by slow dancing. Well I won't even go into all the guilt and shame religion taught me about this! What is a girl to do? Well this girl just told those voices to shut the hell up! Ben stops kissing me and I say, "hey I get to say when you stop." He smiles, and says "I just wanted to look at your face, it's my favorite view." I'm done for! This man's a keeper! "Thank you Ben for making me feel so happy today!" I reach up and kiss him and roll him over and say, "I win!" "Oh you cheated Hannah!" "I did not, I just tricked you." Ok, you can trick me anytime girl!" Things are getting very steamy. I say to Ben, "I want you more than I can tell you, but my heart is not ready, and I'm sorry that I can't right now."

Ben says to me, "you know Hannah, I don't ever want you to feel that pressure from me. If it happens for us, it will be the perfect time. And I'm a patient man, so I'll wait. I think you'll be worth the wait." The guy is freaking me out. I mean really, can he be this great? "Thanks for understanding Ben. I hope you know it is hard to not continue but, well I just can't." "It's okay Hannah, you don't need to feel bad, you have every right to your feelings." "I know, my friend Ruth would tell me to quit being such a middle child." "What does that mean?" "Well, middle children tend to want to please people and make everyone okay. We sacrifice our feelings for the sake of others feelings. Sorry Ben, I'm getting a little heavy for ya." "No, I think it's cool. That info will help me when I'm making Hannah deals!" We laugh! "Good, glad I could help." "Here's some help for you, I'm a middle kid too!" "Oh, nice to know!" "So that sounds about right, I'm pretty good about people pleasing." We are both laying on our backs on the blanket staring at the sky. "Hey Ben, do you like to find pictures in the clouds?" "That's one of my favorite things to do." "I feel like this is the most perfect day!" "I agree! So what do you see?" "I see a dog, do you see his face? He looks like a poodle." "Oh yeah, I see him. Hey I see a heart! It's perfect!" "I see it! What do you think that means?" Ben asks. "God loves us!" "I'll take that Hannah! It's so easy with you." "I'm glad you think so Ben. But, remember I am a girl and we can have a lot of emotion!" Laughter! "My Dad says men have three emotions. You are either sad, mad, or glad. And that women can have all of those at once!" "That's pretty funny. Your Dad sounds like a wise guy." "He is but, I can't tell him that!"

"Well Hannah, I guess we better pack it up and hike back to the truck." "I know, I just hate that it has to end now." "I did not mean it had to end now, we just need to get back to the truck before it starts getting dark." "You're right." We are still wet and I'm starting to get a little bit chilled. It will feel good to get back to the house and change my clothes. We make our way back to the truck and I'm really cold now. As soon as the sun drops in the mountains, so does the temperature. Back home in the desert it's not as dramatic. We make it to the truck. Ben opens my door and gives me a sweet kiss, and a pat on the butt. Funny thing is, I like his pat. Unlike Evan's. Yuck, I want to delete that out of my thoughts. Oh wow, this feels good to be in the warm truck. "Ok beautiful, let's get you home and into some dry clothes." "Sounds like a plan!" We are both quiet on the ride home, but it does not feel weird. Just peaceful and comfortable. "Ben?" "Hannah?" we say each others name at the same time. "You first Hannah." "Well, just wondering when I will see you again?" "I am hoping in two weeks. I will call and check on you, if it's okay with you." "Of course it is! That will help me get through two weeks with the King!" "I want to help you anyway I can!" "So happy you do. Ben, these have been three, great days! I'm so glad I could not get hold of you that day I was sick." "Me too! Was meant to be Hannah!" "Do you really believe that?" "Yes I do! I believe there are no accidents." "So this is part of our plan?" "Yes it is. So far so good!"

We pull into the driveway, Juanita is still not home from picking up Jack. Ben asks if it's ok to come in, "well yeah!" I say. We get in and I tell him that I'll quickly change. I'm in my room and Ben hollers, "hey I was thinking, would you want to come over to my house tonight?" "YES!" I open my door and love is in front of me! Our lips always find their way to each other. Ben says, "Hannah I want to go home and get things together, because I have to leave early. So can I draw you a map and you come over as soon as you feel ready? I know you have your new job starting in the morning." "Yes I need to do a few things to be ready." "Okay deal! I will see you soon!" "Not too long, I want to look at your face as long as I can." "No worries I will be quick!" He walks out and I feel like I never want to leave him! It's only been three days and I already have such strong feelings for him. I have never felt this for anyone before. My heart feels like it could explode! Hannah, get a grip! I need to focus and finish folding my laundry, and pick out something to wear for work tomorrow. Done! I freshen myself up and head out the door. Oh crap, I forgot my map. Run in to get it. I'm getting in my car and up pulls Juanita and Jack. So I hop out to hug Jack and tell Juanita my plan. "Oh I missed you buddy!" "I missed you Hannah!" "I can't wait to hear all about your time with Dad, but I have to go now." "Will you be back to read to me?" "No, I'm sorry. I will tomorrow I promise." "Ok Hannah! My Mommy will have her turn tonight." "Yes she will! So see ya in the morning. Sweet dreams!" Juanita winks at me and says, "enjoy!"

And enjoy I will! I follow the map that Ben drew for me, and up I pull into his driveway. There's his truck, wow! What a cute little place, it's a little A-frame cabin, really cute! I walk up the stairs and onto his deck, I see him through the window walking to the door. He opens it and greets me. Oh I can't get enough of him! No shirt on, and that is okay by me! I hug him and kiss his neck. "I like that," he says. "What a great place you have! I like it." "Perfect for me and my dog Duke." "Where is Duke?" "Out back. You'll meet him. He's mad I didn't take him today. I don't blame him, I wouldn't have wanted to miss it! Well I was not willing to share your attention with him." "I'm glad you feel that way." "I do. Which brings me to something I want to ask you Hannah. I know we have only seen each other for three days but, I just really don't want to see anybody but you! How do you feel about it?" It is freaking me out! "I feel the same way and I just want to be with you. I feel bad for anyone else who would try to go out with me because they would be compared to you, and that would be bad for them. I really like you Ben, and I would love to know you more!" "That is great news! I was hoping you felt the same way but, you never know. I called Nicole and asked her for her opinion. Hope you don't mind." "Oh not at all. It's nice to have someone to bounce things off of." "I just don't want to scare you." "I felt that same way." "Ok then, we have a deal." "Yes Ben, we have a deal!" "Ok. Next thing, I stopped and got some tacos at Don Juan's." "Yum! Ok. Let's eat."

We finish the tacos and they are the most delicious tacos ever. Ben grabs my hand and takes me out back to meet Duke. He is a funny looking dog but has character. Ben's brother got Duke as a replacement for his beautiful German Shepherd that he lost. Ben shared that he was not ready, but his older brother John, surprised him with Duke who is suppose to be a full-blooded German Shepherd. "He is no more a Full-blood German Shepherd than me!" I say. We laugh! "True," Ben says. "He is a great dog and I have grown to love him. Well he is half Shepherd. He looks like a hound dog as well. He has papers, that's even funnier." "Whatever he is, he's sweet." "He really likes you Hannah!" "I like him too!" "Now I'm jealous." 'Oh don't be, I've got room in my heart for you both!" "Ok Mr. Duke, let's feed you so I can focus on Hannah." Duke's fed and Ben takes my hand again and says, "can we lay down together? I promise no funny stuff!" "I can't promise that!" "Oh Hannah, I'll help you stay strong." Yeah sure. We lay down on his bed and we are intertwined like two vines. It is such a peaceful safe place. "Hey Hannah, how about you sleep over? I just want to stay this way all night." "Me too Ben. I have to get up early so I will have you up in plenty of time to get home and dressed for work. Deal?" "Deal!" "I will miss you Ben!" "I'll call you in the evenings." "I'll be waiting! Hey, Ben you said that at times you would be gone a month or two." "Yeah I wondered if you were going to ask about that. Well I live a crazy life style Hannah, so I hope you can hang with me. I'm not always sure about how my calendar will play out." "Okay then, it's one day at a time." "Yes that's the truth, right now I think I'll be back in two weeks."

"Okay then, we'll just see how it goes. I'm hoping for the best!" "Me too beautiful!" The fresh air and the day has made us sleepy. We fall asleep in each others arms. Ben's alarm is going off and we wake to each others faces. "This is the best view I have ever woken up too!" "I'm glad to know. You're a pretty good view yourself! I wish I could rewind and go back three days and do it again!" "That would be nice." He kisses me with such passion, it's like a drug. "Can I have a bottle of your kisses to take with me Hannah?" "Sure! It will cost ya!" "I'll pay whatever!" "I have to figure out a price, so I'll get back to you." "Hurry, time's running out!" "I hate to do this, but I have to get in the shower and be on the road by seven." "Ok. I'll make coffee for you." "Great! One more kiss!" I don't think it will be the last one. I make the coffee. Ben comes out looking cuter than ever! "Here's your coffee, just black right?" "Yes. I don't have any cream Hannah, but I have milk." "Yeah I found it." We finish our coffee and I tell him I've got to go. "I've got a big day ahead of me, and so do you so let's have our final kiss, and say goodbye. This has got to last two weeks, remember? Make it good." Oh, and he did! "You don't disappoint, Ben!" "You neither Hannah! Well good luck today and I'll call tonight." "I miss you already Ben! Be safe on the road! Deal?" "Deal! Love making deals with you! I look forward to a lot more!" "Me too! I guess I'll go now. I've got to get on the road too." We kiss one more time and I walk away to my car. "Hannah!" Ben calls. I turn and say, "what?" He says, "I just wanted to look one more time at my favorite view." I smile and say, "it will be waiting for you." "Ok. I'll call you tonight." "Ok. safe travels! Mizpah!" "What?" he asks. "I'll explain later." "Ok." "It's good Ben!" I laugh to myself and get in my car, he waves and smiles. That smile. That melts me! I honk at him and off I go! Bye Ben! Oh, my heart!

CHAPTER 6

Happy Pants

So excited about this day, I can't wait to work with Dorothy. It makes leaving Ben a little easier, knowing I get to spend time with such an amazing person. I feel like I'm the luckiest girl in the world to get to be mentored by her. As I'm dressing, I am pulling up my pants and think about a conversation I had with my Mother. She said, "you know Hannah, you can choose to put your happy pants on or not." I laugh. As I snap my pants, I say to myself *okay Hannah, you are wearing happy pants today!* I do love my Mom even though we butt heads much of the time, she does have some funny antidotes for life's problems. My favorite is, "there is no need to be mean to ourselves." She is right about that! I do think at times we are just not nice to ourselves. So I want to work on that one.

Off to Shoe Heaven I go! That is such a great name! Lord, give me strength not to buy any! I'm early and Dorothy is not here yet. So I just wait in my car. Oh, here she comes in her Cadillac. She just overflows confidence and beauty. It's a beauty that is beyond outside looks. Can't wait to learn more about that beauty! I get out of my car and walk over to her to see if she needs any help. "Good morning sweet wonderful Hannah!" Oh what a feeling! "Good morning Dorothy! I'm so excited for today!" "Well I was thinking on the way over how excited I am to have you!" "Can I help you carry anything?" "You may carry this bag, please. I'm meeting with my accountant today, so had to bring some extra paper work with me." "Oh I hate paper work!" "Me too Hannah, so let me tell you it is important to have a good accountant when you are in business." "I guess I need one now that I am in business." "I can introduce you to mine today." "That would be great. I just can't afford it yet." "You will soon my dear. I'm going to teach you, and I know already that you will be a good student." "I'm so happy you think so!" "Oh I'm a good judge of character, and I knew the moment I met you that you are special Hannah! Now the biggest thing is you understanding you are!" "Thank you Dorothy!" "Well let's get this party started Hannah!" "I like that attitude." "When you think of your work as that and enjoy, it will not feel like work then my dear. My good ol'Dad taught me that! I miss him!" "I bet, I can't imagine life without my Dad." "Well you must have a great one like I did." "I think so!"

Walking into the shoe store, Dorothy asks me to flip on the lights. Then she says, "follow me to the back, we got a shipment in last week and have not been able to get them all put out yet and organized." "Wow this really is shoe heaven!" Dorothy laughs at me, "oh you make me smile Hannah!" She shows me what she needs me to start doing first. She wants me to organize the shoes by sizes. "This will take you a bit of time, I've got to go in the office and get ready for the accountant. If you have any questions, don't hesitate to come to the office and ask." "Okay sounds great, I'll get busy."

Two hours later, and I'm finished. That is a lot of shoes! I walk to Dorothy's office, she's with the accountant. So I knock and she says, "come on in Hannah." "I am finished Dorothy, what's next?" "Well, you did that fast for your first time!" That's good news I'm off to a good start! "Hannah this is my accountant, Pat." "So nice to meet you, Pat." Likewise Hannah. Dorothy says you'll be needing an accountant soon." "Yes I will." "Well here is my card, please call me if I can assist you." "I will, thank you." "Excuse me Pat, I need to help Hannah for a moment." "No problem." "Follow me Hannah, and I will show you how to open, and Margie should be here any minute. I'll get her to train you on the cash register." "Okay, sounds good. I hope we have a busy day!" "Me too!" "I would rather be busy, it makes the day go faster." "Watch out Hannah, the older you get, you will find time goes much too fast! But, I know what your saying!" We laugh.

In walks Margie, she's a beautiful woman, with the kindest blue eyes and the brightest smile. She says, "well, you must be Hannah. Dorothy has told me so many good things about you Hannah. I'm so happy that you're going to be working with us. Sounds like we're lucky to have you." "No ma'am I think I'm the lucky one, Dorothy has said many kind things about you as well Margie, so I'm just grateful to get to be here and work with you amazing women!" "I like you already Hannah! Anyone who calls me amazing is on my good list! Okay then, let's get you trained up on the cash register and as the day goes by, we'll get you trained in all the different areas. I think you'll be a quick learner though." "Well I hope so, I'm excited to learn." "Hannah, that's what makes the difference in life, those that are excited to learn and willing will be game changers, and those that are not willing will stay in their same place, usually complaining about it." "Well I don't want to be that one!" "I don't think you will, sweet girl."

I see so much of Dorothy and her ways in Margie already. I love that I will be spending time with them, and hoping they will rub off on me!

I can't believe it's five o'clock already! The day flew by. I met some wonderful people, and I think a few will call me for hair appointments. I'm hopeful anyway. Margie and Dorothy tell me that I did great, and are so happy to have me. After Evan, I needed to hear that more than I knew! I clock out, hug the girls and head for home. Can't wait to share my day with Juanita.

Home sweet home, I do love my home here in the mountains. Well Juanita's not home yet. Not sure where she is?

All of a sudden I think of Ben. Wow, I can't believe I really made it through the day and I did not think about him until now. I was just so busy with my new job. But now that I have let him in my mind, I can't wait to talk to him! I hope he calls soon. I think I'll get comfortable and put on my comfy clothes. As I'm doing that, I think about the analogy of comfy clothes and people in our lives that are just like comfy clothes. You know the one's that you can just let it all hang out with, without fear of judgment or disappointment. Those are hard to find and once you do, no matter how raggedy they get you will never let go of them! They are the real deal. I feel so blessed to have Ruth and my Sis. They are my comfy people! Wonder if Ben will be too? We shall see. Oh the phone is ringing, "hello?" "Hey Hannah!" "Is this my far away boyfriend?" "Yeah, it is." "I'm so happy it is you! I was just thinking about you." "I'm glad to hear that! How was your first day at the shoe store?" "Awesome! I swear I had to pinch myself several times. Margie is as wonderful as Dorothy! Makes my time with Evan all worth it for having met those two women." "Well that is good." "Yes it is! How about you?" "It was a crazy start, but it all came together and was good, except I could not quit thinking about you." "Oh that's sweet Ben!" "Well it's true. I'm not sure how I'm going to make it without seeing you." "I know what you mean, I feel the same way. Crazy how fast it is happening.

It kinda freaks me out! I might have to drive back for a look at you." "Come on, I won't fight you on that!"

"Well I'm going to see how the week goes, and maybe I'll sneak up on Saturday, and we can spend Saturday evening and Sunday morning together, and then I'll have to get back." "I would love that! I don't want you to feel pressured but, time with you makes me smile!" "That's my goal in life, to make you smile as much as I can Hannah!" "You're doing pretty good so far." "Also it's Nicole's birthday so we might go out with them for a little while and celebrate." "That sounds good to me. I'm already praying your week is smooth and you come back!" "You're bringing heaven into it." "You know it! Ok I think I'll be there." "Yay! I don't want to go, but the guys are waiting on me to go and eat." "Well ok. You better feed them. Can I call and kiss you through the phone good night?" "You better!" "Ok talk to you later!" "Yes! Bye"

Oh my heart! That man makes me all tingly! Now all I want is his lips, and to look at him. Okay Hannah, pull it together girl! I need to eat as well. I hear Juanita pull in the driveway.

I look out and see Jack running up the stairs, what a happy sight! He swings open the door and screams, "Hannah I'm home and I missed you so much today!" This guy really does own my heart! I grab him in my arms, "I missed you buddy!" He holds my cheeks in his hands and says, "Hannah you're budiful!" "That is gold, I'm budiful! I love you Jack!" "No I love you the mostest Hannah!" "I don't think so Jack." "Yes Hannah!" Juanita says, "not another Jack and Hannah love fest." "Yes Mom!" "Oh, you two are too gooey for me." "Too much sugar for you?" "What are you guys saying?" "Your Mom is saying, you and me are sweet!" We all laugh! What a great day! My heart is overflowing. Hope I can carry this good stuff through my week and survive Evan. Godspeed, on my next two weeks! Except for Saturday, and Sunday Lord! You know!

CHAPTER 7

Survival

Survival, that's what I intend to focus on for the next two weeks! I'm off to work with a knot in my stomach, called Evan. I talked with Ruth last night and I just keep thinking about what she said. "Don't give him that power Hannah! Be your happy, Hannah-self and enjoy the people that are positive, and good and let him slide off of you like water off of a ducks back." Oh I do love Ruth's pep talks! Ok. I'm a duck! I think about that for a moment and I hear the voice of truth say, *ducks have a special oil over their feathers that keeps water from soaking into their feathers, you have an oil too and you're under my wing child. You're safe, go with courage and strength.* I feel a warm calm come over me. And then I remember a verse out of the *Bible* from my childhood. *You prepare a table before me in the presence of my enemies: you anoint my head with oil; my cup runs over. Surely goodness and mercy shall follow me all the days of my life.* Funny how that memory showed up. I need to find my *Bible* and find that verse. So I do have oil that protects! I feel courage and strength! I can do this! The Rocky theme song is playing in my head. I laugh to myself. Okay Hannah, another day at the office and plus I work a half-day at Shoe Heaven. Plus I get to see Polly and Rosie today. I'm going to find the good. My Dad would tell me, "Hannah write a list of the good and the bad, and I know the good list will always be longer and stronger than the bad one." Oh Dad, I need to call him! I will, and tell him I hate to admit it but, he is a smart guy! I just don't want to give him a "big head" as he would say to me, "Hannah girl, don't go getting big headed now!" Not me Dad!

So I throw my things in the car and I'm off. I do have a peace and calm about it. I pull up and Evan's not here yet. I must say, I'm happy about that. I go and get everything ready to go for the day, coffee is brewing, I sweep, fold some towels and I'm ready for Polly and Rosie. I wonder where Evan is? Oh well, he is usually here by now.

I see the sisters coming up the sidewalk. They are arm in arm. I just love how they care for each other. Makes me miss my Sis. I'm going to have to go home and see her soon! It has been too long.

The door opens and in they walk. "Well good morning Hannah," they say in unison. I say "good morning girls! I sure have missed you, I couldn't wait to see you this morning!" "We sure have missed you, and look at our hair it's obvious it has missed you and is in need of your care." "Well then let's get started, who's going first? "You go Polly, I'll go second. "Well okay then, I'm glad to go first." "Okay let's get you fixed up Ms. Polly." "Sounds good Hannah." "So how are you? "Well dear, I have not felt good for a few days." "Oh no, what is wrong?" "Not sure, but I think being a nurse and all, I am having some vertigo. I see the doctor tomorrow." "Well I sure hope he can fix you up." "Me too! I sure don't like feeling dizzy and it makes me a little nauseous too." I lay her back and she get dizzy so I shampoo her fast. I begin to share all about Ben with them.

I tell them how crazy I am about him and what a wonderful guy he is. I also share with Polly, that I think he could be my grand man like her Pete. Polly says, "well I'll pray for that Hannah, nothing would give me greater joy than to know you got a grand man just like my Pete! Every girl deserves that!" "Thank you Polly." I continue to share. I tell them the only thing is that he works out of town and is gone a lot. But, you know the old saying, I say, "being apart make the heart grow fonder. Right?" "Well," Rosie pipes in and says, "well honey I hate to tell you this, but in Mississippi where we come from, the black folks say that it makes the heart go yonder. I'm not saying it will but, they did have it right a lot. So just beware, that's all. I just don't want you to be hurt." "Well thank you." "Now don't go get her all worked up Rosie! My Pete and I were apart lots because of the Army and we grew stronger!" "I'm not trying to upset you Hannah and I'm sorry if I did upset you." "Oh I understand, you just care and want good for me. I do have my concerns about it. I will be cautious." Polly says, "well don't be so cautious, you don't enjoy yourself by worrying about something that has not happened. Hannah, life is full of risks honey, so what I know is that anything worth having has a risk to it. Don't miss out because of fear of being hurt. When we love, it will hurt at times. Believe me I thought I would die, when I got the news of my Pete's death. Oh how I hurt Hannah. But honey, the joy of loving that man far out weighed any pain I endured in losing him. I would not have ever wanted to miss out on loving Pete and being loved by him." Oh tears are flowing down my cheeks.

"Oh my little Hannah, I didn't mean to make you cry honey." "That's okay, that's just such a sweet, sweet love story. You and Pete. I do pray that I get that love someday. I'm grateful you shared that with me." "Now don't I feel like a heel," says Rosie. "I sure didn't mean to be negative Hannah, love is a wonderful thing but we will get hurt. I guess I'm just protective of you honey, you're just such a sweet girl. I just don't want to see you ever be hurt but Polly's right, love will hurt sometimes. We have to take the good and the bad." "That is so true." "I hope I haven't made you doubt." "I am going forward with Ben." "The story will unfold and hopefully it will be one of good love," Polly says. "Yes I hope!" I finish up with Rosie's hair. Off the sisters go, arm in arm again. Oh I love them!

Well next up is Harold, my first haircut as a professional. I just love Harold, he is such a kind man. He is one of those people that just drips of Gods goodness, but never says a word or preaches, he just lives it. You feel loved and encouraged in his presence. "Good morning Hannah." "Good morning Harold, how are you?" "Well Hannah, if I got any better I don't know what they would do with me honey!" "That's good to hear Harold! You want your same haircut?" "No I want some added to the top!" I laugh! "What's so funny Hannah?" "You, Harold!" "Ok. I guess if you can't add to the top, then I'll take my good ol'cut you do." "Minus the blood, right?" "Now you're the funny one. Hannah! I tell people the girl will sacrifice blood for you! She's a keeper, I tell them." "I wish everyone was like you Harold!" "Well I don't know about that, Hannah." "I do! You're the keeper!" "Speaking of keeper, my wife wanted me to make her an appointment with you. She wants to meet this wonderful Hannah, and she has not been happy with her hair for a while."

"Well alrighty, I hope I don't disappoint!" "I don't think you will. Evelyn really is easy to please. She's just a little frustrated, I guess the girl who's been doing her hair is just a little flaky, she says she's up and down." "Okay let's get her scheduled, and we will reschedule you for your haircut. Don't forget Harold I will be in my new location next time." "*The Hair Tamer*, right?" "Yes you got it." "I will see you there! Evelyn will see you on

Thursday." "Ok!" He gives me a big hug! "Good job Hannah." "Thanks Harold. I'll work on the top thing. If I get that figured out I'll be a millionaire!" "That is for sure! I hope you do honey." "Me too! "Have a great week!" "You too!"

Now I'm starting to get concerned, Evan's not showed up yet. It's really weird, and of course I know he's on purpose not calling to tell me he's not coming in, just to show me. I am so very tired of this game. Focus Hannah! What a great day so far! I am so glad that Harold's wife will be coming to me. She has to be great too! I am excited for my future!

Oh, the phones ringing. I pick up, "hair shop, can I help you?" "Oh hey Hannah, is Evan there?" It's Carrie, Evan's girlfriend. "No he has not come in yet." "Oh, ok. Well I guess tell him to call me." "Ok I will. How are you?" "I'm sad." "Oh no, I'm sorry to hear that. Anything I can do?" "No, but I'm sorry about you and Evan. I hate you're leaving." "Thanks, but it's for the best." "Evan really is a good guy." "Well I'm sorry, I have missed that part of him. I really did try." "I know that. He just pushes people away." "I can agree with that." She begins to cry, "like he is doing to me." "Oh I'm so sorry Carrie."

"What's wrong, Carrie?" "We just got into a fight and he was upset. I haven't heard from him so, I thought he was supposed to be at work this morning. He usually is there by now." "Yeah, I thought it was crazy that he wasn't in yet but, you know he's not checking in with me. I wish I could give you some advice Carrie, but I just don't know what to tell you about Evan." "I know Hannah, and I don't want to put you in the middle anyhow. I do want you to know that Evan really talked highly of you, and he really did think you were a great hairstylist and worker, and just a good person." "Well you could've fooled me! I'm sorry Carrie, Evan complimented me once the entire time I've worked for him, and has been nothing but negative and actually mean at times. Believe me I tried to look for the good and stay positive, and I thought maybe that he would soften a bit but it never happened. I just can't let myself be treated badly anymore by him. It took me a while but, I do know that I deserve better than that! I don't know what your relationship is with Evan but I do hope that if it's more negative than positive, you will come to see you're a treasure, and deserve to be treated as one." "Well thank you Hannah." "It's true, you're a good, kind person Carrie. I need to stop because I know you love him and I don't want to cross a line I should not. And besides, I need to get ready for my next customer. I will let Evan know you called and I hope that everything works out for the best." "Thanks Hannah! I am sorry I sure did not want to put you in a uncomfortable place." "It's okay Carrie, I know you were not trying to do that. You take care." "You too Hannah, and I wish you the best." "I receive that Carrie! Thanks!"

I hang up the phone, and ponder that conversation for a moment. I think to myself, do some people just think they don't deserve good in life, and they just push it all away? I just don't understand him. He's got this great girl and it seems like he treats her as badly as he treats me, and I just don't get it. Oh well, maybe some things I'll never get. I can't help but wonder.

My next customer coming in is, Ben's brother. Josh's girlfriend, Nicole. I'm so excited to get to visit with her, I haven't seen her since we all went out. I'm cleaning up and I hear the door open. I think it's Nicole but it's not, it's *the King*. I look up and say, "oh hey there, good morning." He replies, "is it?" "Well for me it is so far." "Look Hannah, I'm just gonna be straight with you. I don't need your Polly-anna shit this morning!" "Okay, I'm gonna be straight with you, I don't need your negative shit this morning." "If you'd like honey, be done today!" "You know what? Let's not do this Evan, you do your work, I'll do my work and let's just get through this, okay? You only have nine more days. Let's just try and be professional about this, we do have customers and they deserve our best. So can we have a truce?" "Ok." "Thank you." I see Nicole coming up the walk. She walks in, and wow, Evan is Mr. Charm now. I just shake my head and roll my eyes. He is flirting with her! Oh, I'm going to be sick, and Nicole looks like she might be too. She is beautiful though, she has thick hair down to the middle of her back, and it's a shiny golden brown. And she has the most beautiful brown eyes, and those eyelashes most girls would die for. She is the girl that wakes up and looks beautiful in the morning. You kind of want to hate her, but you can't because as pretty as she is on the outside, she's that pretty on the inside. Funny thing, I only spent an evening with her but you can just feel that from her. So I'm excited to get to know her better. I don't think I'm wrong about her. I hope to be good friends.

Nicole sits down in my chair and I ask her what she's thinking about with her hair. She says, "oh I would love to do a whole new look but, Josh loves my hair long and he would freak out if I cut it so I guess we're just gonna trim it today." "Okay," I say, "we will work on him and one day get you a new do! I wish I had your hair!" "No you don't, it is a pain to dry or do anything with but wear it like this." "How about I do a cool braid on you today? That could be a little change." "I would love that!" Nicole tells me she is excited for Ben and I! "Oh Hannah, he has had some bad ones! I want you to be aware his old girlfriend is still wanting him back." "Ouch!" I say. "Oh don't worry! I just wanted you to know about her. I would want you to do the same for me." "Well thank you, but who is she?" "Her name is Vicky, we call her sticky Vicky!" "That's pretty funny, I'm only gonna guess what that means." "Yeah, I think you can figure it out. Ben is just too nice and she works all the angles." "Well he has never said anything about her to me." "Really? Don't tell him anything I said. I don't want him mad at me." "Don't worry I won't." "You just seem like a great girl, and I don't want any thing or one, to mess it up for you two."

"Anyhow, she works at a little shop downtown called *The Aspen Tree,* just be aware." "Good to know, I don't think she knows about me yet." "Well as soon as she does, honey, the claws will come out I promise you. I know that about her." "Great just what I need more drama. I'm telling you I just am so sick of drama." "Well girl, you're in a small town, there's a lot of drama here." "I guess I better get used to it and keep my big girl panties on!" "You got that right!" We laugh! "I want us to get together, just us girls." "I would love that! I have my roommate, but she has her son and is very busy, so it's hard to do anything together. I miss my best friend back home so I would love to have a girlfriend to hang out with here! Plus you know Ben well, so you might help me with him!" "I would love to help!" "So, can I just ask you how come you and Vicky were not friends?" "That's a story, let me just put it in a nutshell for you. She was always causing Josh and I to get into fights. Josh is kinda jealous, and she knew he was, so it seemed every time we went out together she would cause some sort of weird deal and make Josh think I was flirting with other guys. She reminds me of those soap opera girls that get a kick out of causing problems for other people. At first she draws you in and you think she's cool, but you soon find out she's a mean girl! That is putting it nicely! I just had a thought, *The Aspen Tree* is just across the street from *The Hair Tamer.*" "Oh, it is? Well what made Ben like her?" "I'm telling you, she knows how to work it." "I hope he is really over her." "Oh I think he is."

I finish Nicole's hair; she says "oh Hannah I love my hair, and the braid is awesome! You're so talented I wish I had a talent like you." "Oh you do Nicole, God has put his creation in all of us, but we have to seek and find it. What is your passion?" "I guess maybe that's the problem, I'm not sure what it is." "Yeah, I know what you mean. I felt that way too. So I feel like we may do things thinking it's our purpose and find our passion on the way.

Life is a journey and it will not always be what we plan. But, I have always felt inside of me that it will be okay." "I like that Hannah! You're wise." "I don't know about that! I just know we all have been given God's spirit, and that is the defining thing for us all." "What do you mean? Will we accept it or reject it?" "I call it the voice of truth. I feel like there is so many voices calling to us in this world, but there is only one voice of truth. That is God, and He always brings peace and encouragement and a joy that I can't explain. It's not religion! I'm not saying don't go to church but what I'm saying is, it's personal. Church sometimes does more damage than good, because we feel condemnation. We judge each other's journeys." "That is true Hannah. I want nothing to do with it because of the way I felt there. I always felt bad about myself!" "Right, me too! My Dad said something to me not long ago that I keep thinking about. He said, "Hannah girl, if you go to church for the people you will always be disappointed, but if you go to meet with God, you will never be disappointed!" So I think I may try that!" "Well maybe I will try it with you." "Ok. We'll think about it." "Not sure where I would go." "Well anyway, sorry I didn't mean to preach." "I liked it Hannah." "Well it's really just me searching."

"Don't you think we're all searching?" "Yeah, but sometimes in all the wrong places. Here I go, sounding like a country song!" "You make me laugh Hannah I love that about you!" "You're so encouraging Nicole! The world needs more of you! "We are good for each other!" "I hate it but, I have to get back to work. I will see you this weekend and we will get a plan for some girl time." "I'm in! Thanks again Hannah love my hair and our talk!" "You're welcome! Have a great week!" "You too!"

She leaves, and *the King* says to me, "so who's your cute friend?" Really? I think to myself. "She is a friend's brothers' girlfriend." "Oh bummer," he says, "all the good ones are taken." Once again I'm in shock! Just when I think he can't do it to me anymore, he does. "Oh yeah, by the way I did tell you Carrie called and wanted you to call her back." "No you didn't." "Oh sorry." Then he says, "she can just see what it is like without me, I'm not calling her." Oh my gosh! I'm not getting sucked in to his junk. So I simply answer, "Ok." I can tell it is bothering him that I won't play his crazy game! I feel like I made a giant step for mankind just now! Walking on the moon! Haha!

CHAPTER 8

Changes

I'm so glad it's Friday! The week has gone faster than I thought it would. So grateful. I need to get a gift for Nicole. I am praying Ben gets to come home, I really miss him! My mind is a crazy place at times. I'm stopping to check out *The Hair Tamer* and see what it looks like so far. I pull in and look across the street, looking to see if I see Vicky which is funny, because I have no idea what she looks like. I have not said a word to Ben, because I don't want to throw Nicole under the bus. I figure if we are supposed to talk about it, it will come up. I feel a little nervous about her. I do hope he is done with her. Ok Hannah, focus. Back to why you're here. I get out of my car and walk in to *The Hair Tamer*. "Oh hey Hannah!" "Hey Carla! Wow this is looking great!" "I think so too! Best of all I think we will be ready for you to move in on time." "Awesome!" "How's it going?" "It is what it is. I'm just staying in my space and doing my thing, trying to ignore Evan and his world." Well good for you. I have had some calls for you." "Really?" "I have told people when I would be here. Well, some have heard about you, and some were people you met at *Shoe Heaven* that want to schedule with you when you're here. See I told you Hannah, it would not be long before you could live off the beauty shop." "You were right!" "I did have a girl by the name of Vicky who works across the street at *Aspen Tree*, come by asking lots of questions about you." Oh no, a knot in my stomach. "She didn't want an appointment. She wanted your number but I told her I could not give anything but your work number out." "Oh thank you Carla." "Do you know her?" "No I don't, but I just heard about her. It wasn't good either. I'll tell you later."

"Okay you've got my curiosity up, but I'll wait to hear. So if you want to bring a book by I can start scheduling things for you if you'd like, if not, you can wait until you get here." "That sounds great, I'll have to get another book because I still need mine but, I'll get one this weekend and bring it by." "Alrighty then, I can't wait 'til you're here working beside me." "Me either! I better run, I've got to get to work. I'll pop by tomorrow with my book." "Sounds good, see ya then." "Ok see ya!"

What a refreshing place, I just love how it feels when I walk into that shop. Carla is just such a great person. I just had a funny thought, she has had the same color of hair for a week now. I will have to tease her about that. I guess I should spice myself up a bit, but I'm just so afraid. I don't want to lose my hair, I've seen it happen. Some people overdo their hair, and it just fries...and actually Carla's does look a little fried. She's so beautiful though, she can wear fried hair! I'm trying my best not to think about Vicky and Ben. I wonder why Ben never said anything about her? Well I guess he might feel like that would bother me. I'm going to try and stay positive about this whole thing. Ben is crazy about me!

Here I go, back to the jungle! Well at least I have green on today! Making myself laugh. I'm so glad I can humor myself! I think I'm funny, even if no one else does. Well Ruth thinks I'm funny! I miss her!

Another positive today, it's Dorothy's day to get her hair done with Evan, so that always positive. Plus I get to do Wilma's hair today which always makes me nervous, but I just love Wilma and her fun expressions on life. I walk in, "hey Evan." "Hey." he says back. He has a client in the chair. He is an older gentleman, nobody I know. Evan does not offer to introduce us, so I say, "hello I'm Hannah, nice to meet you." He says, "so you're the Hannah that Dorothy so highly speaks of." "Well that makes me happy to hear." "I'm her other half, Jim. It's a pleasure to meet you young lady." "The pleasure is mine Jim." *The King* is not feeling the pleasure. Oh well. "I'm so glad to get to meet you Jim, I have to get to work now." "Hope to get to know you better Hannah." " Hope to know you better too. I love your wife!" "Yes she is a dandy!" How cute, I think to myself, older people have the cutest way of saying things. "A dandy, I hope to be someone's dandy someday too!" "See, there we already agree on something Hannah." "Well that was an easy one Jim!" "True. But, I think it's a great start." "Me too! Here comes my client I better get ready." In walks Katie, my only compliment Evan ever gave me. "Good morning!" Katie half smiles at me, and kind of mumbles, "good morning." "Come sit Katie." I put the cape on her, and ask her how things are. "That's a loaded question." She starts crying uncontrollably! "Oh no!" I say, and hug her as she just sobs. You know the cry where you are gasping for breath? This is what school can't teach you! So I just let her cry for a bit. Good thing I'm not pressed for time .

In between her sobs, Katie says "I'm sorry Hannah, I'm so sorry I know you don't have time for this, I should have cancelled. But, I have to be honest I just felt like you were a safe place for me to come and talk, and I just so badly need someone to talk to." "I'm glad you feel that way. So tell me what is going on?" "You know last time I was here, I was having troubles with my boyfriend." "Yes. Oh and by the way everyone loved my hair!" "Oh good!" "Anyhow, I thought we had worked things out and all was good." "So?" "Well Hannah, I'm pregnant! He is so mad and said to me that I planned it, and he is not going to be tricked into marriage!" "Wow, Katie! I'm so sorry he said that! Words are tough, once said they can't be taken back, and can leave a big wound. I can feel you're wounded." "Oh Hannah, I am and I'm scarred! My Momma and Daddy are going to be so disappointed in me! They never liked Jared in the first place and warned me that he wasn't a good guy, but I just felt like they couldn't see the things that I saw in him." "Yes I understand, I had a boyfriend like that and I just felt like my parents were constantly looking for everything wrong with him. Katie, everyone has good in them but we get to choose whether we want to see things positive or negative, we all have that ability. You can't make some people see good when all they're looking for is bad. I don't have the answer for you. My Dad has always said to me when it comes to matters of the heart, no one can tell you what to do. I think we know deep down Katie, what we need to do but, it's hard to do." "I know this Hannah, I'm going to have this baby with or without him!" "So see, you have already made a decision!"

"Oh Hannah, thank you so much. You have such a way of just making me feel like everything's gonna be okay. I'm just so grateful to you!" "I know it might not be easy Katie, but I know it will be okay. I just feel better after talking about it with you." "I'm glad Katie! Not sure I helped but, I will always listen." "Yes, and that is what I needed." "Let's get your hair cut, wow has it grown! Pregnancy will cause lots of things to grow girl, get ready!" We laugh! "I so needed this today Hannah! Thank you!" "Anytime Katie!" "Once again I love it Hannah! It is amazing to me how time in the beauty shop can change my perspective and attitude! It's a miracle! Jesus in the beauty shop! Now that is some good news!" Laughter! I write my home phone number down and give it to Katie. "Please if you need anything, don't hesitate to call me! I mean it!" "I will Hannah! Please pray for me to have courage to tell my parents." "I will. They love you and that will cover you." "You're right, I just hate that they will have to hear the negative talk. Do you know how the south is, Hannah? I will be a disgrace." "Well you are not Katie. I hate how the world picks and chooses what is a disgrace. I promise everyone has fallen short of perfect. Only one man I ever heard of, that was Jesus. And He would not condemn you!" "I love that! I will think about that." "Me too! We will fall from time to time Katie. I think God will always use it for good. We have to seek, and when we do we will find. You have been chosen to have one of His greatest miracles, one of his children. Don't be scared, he will take care of you."

"Hannah I never thought about it that way, that is such a cool way to think about it. I'm having one of God's children." "Yes you are I can't wait to meet that little person!" "I'm so excited now! I came in here feeling like the world just crushed me, and now I just feel excitement about my future and about this little miracle I'm carrying!" "It's just changing our focus and our thoughts on what is good, and true and beautiful! It really is a simple thing but it's hard for us to do sometimes, that's why God gives us each other. We pick each other up and speak love over one another." "Well I feel loved Hannah! I'm so glad I found you! You are more than just a hairstylist!" "You are good for my self-esteem Katie!" "I'm so glad I didn't cancel today!" "Me too!" "I have my first doctors appointment today!" "Let me know how it goes." "I will." We hug and off she goes with a smile! That was the best payment ever.

Evan walks into my space, and I guess there's just something about Katie that makes him want to give me compliments. He says, "I couldn't help overhearing Hannah and what you said to her, it was really good." "Well thank you." "You're welcome." Out he walks. I shake my head and think to myself, what's it all mean? Funny thing is, we can be so clear on what others need, but crash and burn when it comes to our own needs. I just preached a sermon, and I hope I will take my own advice and listen to the voice of truth.

I see Dorothy coming up the walkway and just the sight of her makes me smile, she just has such a way about her. She is sunshine. I now have that song playing in my head now, *I've got sunshine on a cloudy day when it's cold outside I got the month of May. I guess you say, what can make me feel that way. My girl!* Dorothy! That will be playing in my mind all day! I will have to share that with her. In she walks. "Hi there!" "Hi," I say, as I go to hug her. "You are the best hugger Hannah!" See, she always has a good thing to say. I want to be like that. "Well you are very huggable!" *The King* rolls his eyes. "I hate to break up the love fest, but we gotta get started on you Dorothy." "Well okay if you must," she winks at me. I still wonder about why she keep going to Evan. Well he does do her hair well. Look at me staying positive! That's not easy with *the King*.

In walks Wilma, and oh my her hair is big today! Actually it's huge! Not sure how she gets it in the car! "Well how's it going girl?" I tell her all about Ben and tell her I need her to pray that he gets to come home tomorrow! "Well, you know I'm on it." "I do, that's why I asked. So let's talk hair." "Oh you know, I want my jet black color. I mean look at these roots girl!" I start putting on her color and she says to me, "I am just wiped out this morning!" "Have you been working hard?" "Oh girl I always do, but it's not that. My Charlie thought we were teenagers again, and we had what I call Olympic sex! I love it, but I might have to join the gym to keep the pace. 'Cause Lord knows, I want to keep my Charlie happy!"

I am just laughing inside of myself, she just blurts these things out like there's no one else here. Evan and Dorothy are around the corner and another woman is waiting on Evan. So funny how people will talk in the beauty shop, as if they are the only ones in here. And Wilma does not have a soft voice, it carries. I'm pretty sure the next door neighbor's can hear. Which makes me think, oh my goodness I can't even imagine what Olympic sex sounds like. Hannah don't go there! "Well Charlie and you have something special," I say. 'Cause I don't really know what to say. "You got that right Hannah, I told Charlie this morning we might just blow each other up one of these days with our passion!" It's so hard sometimes to keep a straight face at some of the things she says. But, I do feel her though, I feel like Ben and I have a strong physical attraction. I tell her that. She says to me, "girl you better have it all! I mean Charlie is my best friend, my partner in crime, and I'll say, it was a crime this morning!" We both burst out laughing! "Wilma I love how you describe things." "I hope I don't embarrass you or make you uncomfortable. Charlie says if I think something I say it. Which he loves about me but, he says for some it can be too much information. You know what I mean?" I do. "You don't make me uncomfortable. I wish I could be more like you. You are true to who you are and that is refreshing! I feel like so much of the time we are all trying to be who we think people want us to be, and we lose who we are. You know what I mean?"

"Oh, don't I know what you mean Hannah. I see it all day long all the time, people being so artificial with each other." "Well it makes me wonder where does it come from? Why do we feel like we can't just be ourselves? I think about children and how they're just happy with who they are, until the world starts telling them *that's not right, you can't be like that, why would you think that, why would you say that? Quit your day dreaming!* On and on." "Oh, you're right honey, but it is a human condition to want to please." "That's what I have always admired about Dolly Parton, she is who she is and you can like it or not. It's okay to want to be pleasing, just not if it's at the cost of you." "So girl, you stay true to yourself!" "I try. I'll tell you Wilma, I love my Mom but she is one who does make me doubt at times, who I am. I don't have her taste in fashion, I guess I take after my Grandma in that way, but she always says, *Hannah you need to fix up more and quit being so plain. You are so pretty if you would only put some pizzazz in your look!*" "Well Hannah, I had the opposite of you, my Momma would always say you look like a two cent hooker waiting for change. How's that for building up self esteem?" "Ouch Wilma!" "You know what I did Hannah? I would look myself in the mirror everyday and say, *I am Wilma Faye Walker and I am beautiful!* I still do it! The best part though is I always here a voice inside say, *yes you are child!* I believe that voice is God!" "That is great Wilma, I am going to start telling myself that too! I hope I hear that voice whisper back at me too." "Oh you will girl, just listen."

"Well honey, I hate to have to rush off but I have to get to the bank. I loved our visit today and I love my hair! You're getting the hang of it." "Sounds like we need to switch Mothers. I got pizzazz and then some!" "My Momma would love your style. She would say if she knew you why don't you dress more like Hannah and tone it down." Well you and my Mom do have the same hair color, Wilma." "Oh that's funny! God gave them us for a reason only he knows." "One thing I know, there ain't no perfect Mothers! Lots pretend to be!" "Hannah you're perfect at being you, stay true honey!" "You too!" "Oh you know I will girl." "See ya at The Tamer next time." "Yes ma'am!" I am proud as I watch her walk out to her car! That hair is touching heaven! Hallelujah!

Long day, I'm tired, ready to get home and I hope Ben calls tonight with good news! I am thinking I will just give Nicole a gift certificate for her hair for her birthday. I'll ask Juanita what she thinks about that idea. Dorothy walks back and says, "Hannah, Jim and I would love to have you to dinner tomorrow night." "Oh Dorothy, I have plans." "Ok. How about Sunday night?" "That will work." "Jim loved you! I told him he would." "You are so kind. Can I bring something?" "No just you. I will draw you a map to my house." "Perfect I was just going to ask how to get there." "Don't you just love that Wilma?" "You know her?" "Yes, from *My Sisters Place*. I think everyone knows Wilma." "Some don't know how to take her at times but, I think she is a hoot!" "Me too! Well I hope her and Charlie don't blow themselves up!" We laugh! I guess everyone heard that! Yep! Oh the things you hear in a beauty shop! Never dull, that's for sure!

Driving home from work, I just chuckled to myself about this day and how much I'm enjoying discovering the new pieces of myself in the people that I'm serving. I am finding things about myself that I never knew until now. I think about the reflection we see in the mirror, and as we share more and more, we begin to reflect with each other. Oh Hannah, you're getting deep. Chuckle!

Home sweet home! Juanita and Jack are gone this weekend. It always feels a little weird when they are not here. I miss them. I just sit and stare out the window running the day's events in my head. The phone rings and startles me! I jump up to answer it. "Hello." "Hey Hannah!" "Just what I was hoping for!" "I like hearing that! What's going on?" "Just home from work and relaxing. Was a busy day and full of emotion. I feel extra tired I guess from the emotional part of it." "What happened?" "Oh, one of my clients is pregnant unexpectedly." "Oh wow!" "Yeah. Anyhow how's your day?" "Crazy day too! Everything that could go wrong, did." "Oh man, I hate that." "So here is the good news I am crazy about you!" "That makes me smile!" "Bad news is, I don't think I can come back." Oh my heart just sank, but I try to keep my big girl panties on. "I'm bummed but, I understand." "Well you're doing better than me. So are you still going out with Nicole and Josh?" "Yes I am. I did Nicole's hair this week and we are like soul sisters." "I knew you two would click." "We are going to start hanging out and having some girl time." "That sounds good." "I need it! I miss Ruth and my sis bad! So Nicole could save my life!" "I thought I was your life saver." "Well you are but, a good girlfriend is gold!"

"So then, what am I? Silver?" "Oh let's not do this Ben, you are on a whole different level." "Okay I will go with that." "It's going to be a lonely weekend, Juanita and Jack are gone and so I'll be home alone." "What? I am really bummed now! I am sitting here just tasting you Hannah!" "Well you know you can't get satisfaction until you get what you're craving." "I want you so bad, I feel like jumping in my truck right now!" "Please do!" I laugh! "Oh Ben we can't do this." "What? Get all hot and bothered over the phone?" "Yeah!" "Alright. So call me tomorrow before I go out." "Of course." "Well I'm kissing you through the phone." "I wish!" "Have a good night!" "You too! Bye!" Oh my heart! It's a real problem for me. This long distance thing is hard! I think about what Rosie said about the heart going yonder, I hope not. Oh well, I think I will take a bath and call Ruth.

I'm in heaven. Nothing better then a hot bath! When life is rough, my Grandma always says take a hot bath. I asked her one time, "why do you always want me to bathe when I have a problem, Grandma?" She said, "because it relaxes you and calms your mind child, and a calm mind produces good thoughts and that makes life better. So your problem does not feel as big anymore." I love my Grandma and sure do miss her and her cooking. I miss Sunday dinner! Oh the yeast rolls and her chocolate cake, and lemon meringue pie. I need to go home soon! I'm feeling a giant hole where my family belongs. I have never been away this long. I am getting a plan for a trip home. It's only a couple of hours away, but it might as well be across the world. When you have barely enough money to get by, there is no extra for gas to go home. I could ask my Dad for money, but I don't want to. I want to show him, or maybe me, I can do this on my own!

CHAPTER 9

More to *Learn*

I wake up feeling excited about my day! I have two new people today. It'll be fun I hope. I always am nervous for a new customer, I wonder if that will ever go away? Wondering if I can please them, and if they'll be happy with their hair. My thoughts wander to Ben. I'm trying not to be bummed about the news of Ben not being able to come tonight. I am looking forward to more time with Nicole and Josh and the rest of their friends, they're a pretty great bunch. Oh well, it is what it is. I'm going to roll with the punches. I better get with it and go to work.

Back at Evan's kingdom. In walks my first customer, she works with Nicole at the bank. Her name is Sheila, and she's one of the loan officers. A pretty lady, a little to the chubby side. She is dressed very professionally. I introduce myself, and she says, "you have made a good name for yourself Hannah." "Oh thank goodness," I say! "Yes remember you're in a small town, so it is best to keep it that way." "I'm trying." "Well so far so good!" "Thanks for letting me know Shelia." "I'm honest, so you won't get any bull from me." "Okay I like that. Let me get you started." I ask her what she would like and she says, "I like long feathered layers, a lot like Farrah Fawcett." "Ok. I get that a lot. I wish I could have that hair myself. Don't have the hair for it but, you do." She tells me she has a date tonight and hoping to get lucky! I smile and think, wow that is something I think of men saying. It's a new day! Women wearing the pants and saying what they want, she wants some good sex. I ask her if she thinks he might be the one for her. She answers me, "well I'll let you know after I see what he does to me!" Oh my, I still have lots to learn!

Get Sheila finished up, her hair looks awesome! She re-schedules with me. Thank goodness, I'm so glad that she likes her hair. The first time you do someone's hair it's always a little nerve-racking. When they say it looks great, they love it, you breathe a sigh of relief. "Enjoy your date tonight, I hope you get lucky!" "Me too Hannah!" Out the door she goes feeling sexy! Oh boy I did not see that one. She looks like this serious professional women, and inside her is a sex kitten! Who knew! I do love how we think we know people just by their outside appearance, then find out they are nothing like we thought. So I guess that old saying never judge a book by it's cover is the truth. I'm on my last customer of the day and she is another new one. Funny I started the day with the new customer and ending with a new customer. Here she comes up the walkway. She is beautiful! In she walks, "I'm Kathy." "Hello I'm Hannah, nice to meet you. Follow me over here Kathy. Okay, so tell me what your dreaming of." "I want to keep my length, but would love some more layers. Also I want to get in for highlights in a couple of weeks." "I will be moving to *The Hair Tamer* in a week, so I will be there when you come back for color." "Oh, ok. I hope I don't offend Carla. She used to do my hair, but I was not happy with what she was doing." Now I'm feeling nervous! "I don't think she will care that I'm doing your hair, but I can ask her if you would like." "No, you don't need to, I think if it does, she will just have to get over it." I'm confused now. One minute she does not want to offend her and the next she does not care if it offends her. Oh, people! I start to cut Kathy's hair, and she starts telling me how to do it! I bet Carla was relieved that she quit coming to her. She is also very needy of hearing how beautiful she is. It's interesting how she'll says things that make you have to tell her she is amazing and beautiful. She is exhausting to be with. It's all about her! She thinks she is so positive, but really all she does is find everything wrong with everyone and everything. I finally finish her hair and I swear if she says anything is wrong with it, I will tell her it's her fault and she told me how to do it! She says she thinks it's good but, will have to see after she messes with it. "Ok. Well let me know." I'm not sure but, I think that is what you call a narcissist. I will look that up in my dictionary when I get home. She schedules with me for her color. Oh, that will be a tough couple of hours. I'm sure she will direct my every move. I don't feel her loving it, but I don't think she will ever give that satisfaction to me. I am ready for some fun tonight!

Kathy's out the door, and I'm cleaning up my messes, and ready to get home and changed and have me some Hannah time!

I call Nicole to make sure we are still going to Blue Moon. "Hey Hannah, are you ready for some fun?" "Yes I am!" "I'm sorry about Ben not being able to come." "Me too!" "But, we are going to celebrate you!" "I'm excited! I'm ready to dance!" "Me too! See you at the Blue Moon at eight." "See ya, bye." The never ending question, what to wear? I wish Juanita was here to get me dressed. I get into the shower and the phone rings of course. I jump out, grab a towel and run for it. Get there and whoever it is hangs up right when I pickup. Dang it! I hate that and then I wonder, was it Ben? Oh well, I hope he calls back if it was. Back to the shower. I finish getting ready. I feel good about my look tonight! Wish Ben could see me!

I pull up to the Blue Moon and it is a full house! Wow, I wonder why it's so busy? Find a parking place finally. It's even early. I see Nicole and Josh pull in, I'm waiting for them. Hope I get in. "Happy Birthday!" We hug. "It has been so far." "That's great!" "Hey Josh." "Hey Hannah, my brother gonna make it?" "No, I don't think so. I never heard from him so I think he is stuck there." "Well he is missing out again. He's married to his job." "Oh Josh," Nicole says, "he is just responsible and wants to do well, nothing wrong with that." "I would not say he is married to his job. Anyhow we are here to have fun! My birthday so I get to run this party!" "You're off to a great start then Nick!" "I love you Josh!" "I love you too!" I love how Nicole handles Josh. We are in and a friend of theirs has a table for us all. There will be twelve of us. I'm feeling a little sad Ben is not here, and then think, is it always going to be this way? Wonder if Josh is right, maybe work is his first love. Oh Hannah, stop you are here for Nicole. So have fun girl. Josh gets us all a drink. Let the game begin. Nicole introduces me to everyone. I feel comfortable with them, so glad to meet new friends. The band is starting and it's Mick's band. I wish Juanita was here. We don't get to do enough fun stuff together.

The parties going great and Nicole comes over to me and says, "hey I have to tell you something, come in the bathroom with me." Okay, sounds serious. We get to the bathroom and Nicole says to me, "listen. Vicky just walked in." "Oh great." I say. "So do you think I should go home?" "No don't let her make you leave, I just wanted you to know that she's here and I'm going to point her out to you. I know her though, she'll come over like she's our buddy, hugging and kissing everybody. I just wanted you to be ready for her. You never know with Vicky." "I have a stomach ache now, I hate this." "Don't let her ruin your night Hannah." "Well I don't want to ruin your night Nicole, it's all about you girl, your birthday!" "That's the spirit Hannah! Okay let's go back and have some fun!" Oh what a feeling! We get back to the table and Nicole nudges me. It's Vicky doing her thing. She is hugging and licking her lips like she is about to French-kiss someone. She is cute though. I get the name sticky Vicky! Nicole looks at me and rolls her eyes at me as, Vicky hugs her and does the weird lip thing. Nicole introduces me to her and she says, "I have heard about you." "Hope it's good." I say. "Well I hear you are hanging out with my Ben." Wow, did she just call him her Ben? "I didn't know he was yours?" "Well we are taking a break but, we have been together for two years." Feels like I got punched in the stomach! "Well Vicky, I'm not here to figure you and Ben out, I'm hear to celebrate Nicole." Nicole says, "come dance with all us girls Hannah," and saves me from Vicky. "I can't believe she just did that Hannah. I'm sorry she is here but, please don't let her mess up your fun!" "I'm trying." The band starts playing *play that funky music*. I love dancing to this song. The girls go wild on the dance floor! We are having a blast and even forgetting about Vicky.

The girls are tearing up the dance floor, we're on our third straight song in a row! I am having a blast, until I look out and I see Ben. And hanging on him is Vicky. Please, this is not happening. I don't know what to do. Nicole sees what I'm seeing and looks at me with a confused look. I stop dancing, and tell her I think I need to leave. "Oh Hannah I hate this." "Yea me too but, I think it is best for all if I go. Happy Birthday Nicole! I will leave your gift at your seat." "Ok I'll call you in the morning Hannah." "Don't worry you just have fun. Bye." I head for the table and can feel I'm being watched. Josh gives me a hug and says, "don't let sticky Vicky get to you." "I think the only way that will happen, is if I leave Josh. I had fun. Go dance with the birthday girl." "I think I will. Thanks for coming Hannah, Nicole thinks you're great and it meant lots to her." "Thanks Josh. Bye." I'm getting my stuff and Ben walks over, and I can tell he does not know what to do. The normal thing would be to kiss me, but he doesn't. He says, "hey surprise!" "Yeah it is!" "Where you going Hannah?" "Home." "Why?" "Really Ben? I think it's for the best, enjoy the party." "Hannah wait, can we talk?" "I don't think I can right now." "Please!" "Bye Ben." I can't get out of the bar fast enough! Oh my heart hurts. I'm hurrying to my car and Ben's good friend Bo is standing outside. "Hey Hannah, why you leaving so early?" "Just feels a little weird with Vicky, she said he was her Ben." "Did she? That's crazy Hannah." "Well looking at them in the bar, Ben did not look like he was hating all her attention." "If you knew her you would understand." "Well I think Ben needs to figure it out. I'm done 'til that happens. He never even told me about her. I hate finding things out that he should have shared with me from other people." "Well I can't fix it Hannah, but I do know Ben is crazy about you." "Not feeling it Bo. Thanks for the talk though. See you around Bo." "See ya Hannah."

Fiddling with my car keys, I can't seem to get the key in the lock. I finally do get in my car and as soon as I turn the car on, I just start bawling. This night did not go like I had thought it would. I think to myself, what was I thinking wanting to be a grown-up? I am so ready to turn in my big girl panties. I wish Juanita was here, I sure could use a friend to talk to. I'm sitting in the dark, just staring at the wall. Now I'm thinking why didn't I just let Ben talk to me? Why did I overreact? But, did I overreact? This is hard ,all I want is Ben and now I left him with Vicky. Oh Hannah! I think I'll call Ruth. The phone just rings. Ok. What next? After an hour of sitting here, I decide I will go back and talk to Ben. I'm back at the bar and no Ben. I will go to his house then. I pull up and there are two cars in the driveway. I am pretty sure it's Vicky's car, but I don't want to jump to conclusions so I will go to the door. There is a window and I can see Ben on the couch and Vicky is on her knees in between his legs and looks like she is crying and he touches her face. Ok. I have seen enough. Oh no, his dog starts to bark. I hurry to my car and just as I'm pulling out I see Ben on the deck. Bye Ben! I'm headed home but, all I want is to go home and see my family. I decide that is what I'm going to do. I'm ripping off the big girl panties and being a little girl and running home! Pack a bag, and leave Juanita a note. I call my sis and no answers. Everyone is out having fun, but me. Get in my car and head for home. All I can hear is my Dad saying, what are you thinking driving at midnight by yourself?

Maybe it is crazy but right now I need a life line, and that's my family. I will go to my sister's house and spend the night with her. Tomorrow I will go to grandma's for Sunday dinner with my family, and hopefully gather some wisdom and some healing for my heart. I just remembered I was supposed to go to Dorothy's for dinner tomorrow night, and also I have to work at the shoe store on Monday. I will call Dorothy first thing in the morning and ask for forgiveness and a rain check for dinner and also the day off Monday. It feels good to be driving home. Pulling into my sisters and her light's on, thank goodness. I knock at the door and she asks, "who is it?" "It's your sister, open up." She opens the door, "what in the world are you doing here?" "I'm surprising you!" "You did a good job I was thinking, who is knocking at my door at one-thirty in the morning?" "I tried to call but, no answer." "Oh I went out with my girls. I just got home. So perfect timing. What made you decide to come home at this hour?" "Long story but, has to do with Ben and I just really have been homesick!" She grabs me and hugs me hard! "Oh I have missed you Hannah! Let's get in bed and talk." "Sound good to me! I know it was a crazy thing to take off tonight and drive here but, I'm so glad I did!" We settle in bed and I spill the beans on what happened with Ben. Sis agrees that he should have told me about her. I'm exhausted and so is she. She says, "I'm glad you're home little sister. You're going to be okay! Let's get some rest, that always makes things better." "Grandma would want me to take a bath." We both laugh and drift off to sleep.

I need to call Dorothy, I'm a little nervous but I'm going to do it. Phone's ringing. "Hello?" "Hey Dorothy, it's Hannah. I'm afraid that I have to give you some bad news." "Oh my, what is it Hannah?" "I'm not gonna make it to dinner tonight, but I would love a rain check, and also I want to ask if there's any possibility I could have tomorrow off?" "Oh well I was worried it was something really bad. No problem on dinner I was going to call you because Jim is not feeling well, so a rain check it is and let me call Margie and make sure it's okay with her. So call me back in a few minutes." "Okay Dorothy, I wouldn't ask if it wasn't really necessary. I just really need that day off. But, if it doesn't work I will be there." "Ok. Call me back in ten minutes." "You got it! Thank you." Why did I let that be scary? Dorothy is such a kind, wonderful person! I'll call her back and it will be fine.

Sis and I head out for lunch with Mom. It's so good to see her! "I missed you Hannah!" "I missed you too Mom!" So I begin to share all that I have been doing, and my Mom lights up at hearing about my shoe store job and my discount on shoes! I did get my love of shoes from her! She also wants to meet Dorothy! "You would love her Mom!" "I think so Hannah." "You do love the finer things in life and so does Dorothy! She is amazing!" "We need to make a trip up there," she says to my sister. "I'm ready when you are Mom," she answers. "Please come up! You two can sleep in my room and I will sleep with Jack, or on the couch." "We will make a plan and come up." "It is beautiful there." "Time flies, before you know it a year goes by and it just goes faster the older you get girls!" "We know Mom, you always tell us that." "Well it's true!" "I'm sure it is Mom!" I laugh thinking about how older people will share things over and over with you, even when you tell them they have shared that with you already, they just continue on and share it again. I wonder will I do that too? Probably, it seems to be a thing. "So Hannah, are you going to see your Father and the Baptist whore?" "Come on Mom, don't go there! We are having a great time. The baptist whore is my Dad's girlfriend." Yes she is still bitter and I don't see better coming yet. I will pray for a miracle! "I will see Dad at Grandma's, not sure about Cookie." "That name, what is it short for?" "I don't know Mother."

"It sounds like a stripper name to me." "I'm sure it does Mom! Let's move on. Have you had any dates?" "Well I do have a man I would like you girls to meet. We shall see but, I am enjoying his company. He loves to dance and so do I." That's good news! I can't wait to meet him!" Well all and all, lunch was a success! You never know with Mom, she can definitely push my buttons! But, I love her!

"One more thing, Hannah what about your love life?" "Oh mom that's complicated right now." "How so?" So I explain the situation with Ben and Vicky. "Well Hannah, there's lots of fish out there. Sometimes you catch one, and it's not the right one, so throw it back and fish again." "Good one Mom, tell that to my heart." "Your heart will heal my dear." "I hope so. Right now it has no desire to fish again!" "Believe me I know Hannah!" "I know you do Mom." "Well," my sis breaks in, "I have news, Bill asked me to marry him." "What! Why did you not tell us sooner? What did you say?" "I said Yes!" "Oh I'm so happy for you sis!" "Well let's plan a wedding!" "Hang on Mom!" Mother has a way of taking over, and my dear sweet sister has a hard time telling her no. It's her wedding so let's let her plan and we will help. That's all I was wanting to do. "We are in no hurry so it won't be for awhile." "How exciting! Something fun to look forward to! I love Bill and I know he is crazy in love with you sis!" "You don't seem excited, what's wrong?" my Mom asks. "I just have my concerns, that's all." "Well there will always be those. What is your biggest concern?" "His need to party all the time and be out all the time. I love a good time myself but, Bill takes it to a whole other level!" "Yeah, that could be a concern. Don't you think he will out-grow it?" "I hope so, but what if he doesn't?" "Well you can see how it goes, it's not like you're getting married tomorrow." "That's true. I just don't want to make a mistake." "Well honey, there are no guarantees, look at your father and I, twenty-one years! Don't let our marriage effect your choice. We all have our own journey. Everyone's will be different. I'm proud of you for not just jumping in. Take your time, you're still young." Wow Mom! I'm seeing a little hope for better instead of bitter!

Finish up our lunch and I hug Mom goodbye. "I will be up to see you soon Hannah." "I hope so Mom! That was a good visit," I say to my sister. My Mom hollers at my sister as we are getting in the car, "hey Morgan, let me know when you want to start planning!" "Ok." she answers. I shake my head, oh Mother! She can't help herself! We laugh! "Don't you let her take over 'cause you know she will! Be strong and use your no word!" "I will." "You know how she influences you. Not that it's all bad, but, if it is not what you want…" "I know you're right Hannah. I will call on you if she gets pushy." "Ok deal!" We are headed for Grandma's house. I can't wait to see her! I am a Grandma's girl, through and through! She is the person who really sees me, for me. She sees me in a light no one else does. Oh what would I do without Grandma! That I can not even consider! We walk in her house and I feel safe and loved. The smell coming from the kitchen is heaven! She always has a roast with potato's, carrots and the best gravy you have ever had, and her yeast rolls with butter melting over them. Oh that aroma. And then there is her desserts, her chocolate cake is like a party in your mouth you never want to end, and her lemon meringue pie is as Ruth puts it, like angel pee! Not that I know what angel pee taste like but, Ruth assures me it is like my Grandma's lemon meringue pie! The sweetest taste, that always leaves you happy and content! So I'll go with that! But, the best thing is her hug and how she looks at me. My Grandma is like a salve for my soul.

"Hey grandma guess who?" "Get in here, let me look at you girl. Well would you look at my Hannah Marie, you are just beautiful you're looking more grown-up everyday!" "I don't feel like it, this day Grandma!" "Well why not?" "Oh I just thought I wanted to be a grown up, and it turns out that it isn't what I dreamed it would be." "Oh well honey it's not that bad." "I know but, it feels that way. Grandma you have had some really hard things happen to you, how did you not want to just curl up and quit?" "Well I determined that I had a lot to live for and I wanted to live! Those bumps in the road Hannah, God will use to take to a higher, better place. What have I always told you?" "That I have a beautiful basket of apples, and sometimes there is a bad one, and if I focus on the bad one I miss the basket full of beautiful apples!" "Yes my dear, that is the truth! I know it's just seems hard for me right now. Sit yourself down and I will be right back." "Ok." She returns with a paper and pencil and draws a line down the middle. "Okay I want you to write the good stuff in your life on the left side, and the bad on the right side." "Oh Grandma!" "Do it Hannah Marie!" "Alright I will." So I begin and before I know it my left side is filled up, and the right only has two things, well three: Evan, Ben, and Vicky. "Now," Grandma says, "you can't control people, but you can control how you let them effect you." "It's not always that easy Grandma." "I know but, you keep on giving them to God every time they come into your thoughts, you replace the thought with all the good thoughts on this paper and soon you will no longer be held captive by them. Who are you Hannah?" "I am a child of God, who is completely loved!" "That is right and don't you ever forget it!" "I love you Grandma!" "I love you, Hannah!"

Sis and I help Grandma get the table set and get everything ready. Everyone should be showing up pretty quick. I can't wait to see my Dad, I sure have missed him! It's funny how you take for granted all the things that you have on a daily basis and then when you don't have them you realize how special they are. I always have taken my family for granted. This time I realize how much they mean to me and how special time is with them. I am seeing all my beautiful apples. Life is good! In walks my Dad, and behind him my brother, his wife, and two children. Cookie isn't with him. I'm happy about that, I like having my Dad without her. I know that sounds bad, but he is different around her. He loses part of himself. I wonder, is that part of the deal? Must we lose a part of us in order to be part of someone else's life? I hope not. Maybe we settle for acceptance instead of authenticity. I think true love searches for authenticity instead of acceptance. The more I think about it, I see that's probably most of the problem for most relationships. Instead of being our authentic self, we try to fit into the mold of what the other person is expecting. And somewhere along the line we lose ourselves or part of ourselves, and then one day wake up screaming because we're not being true to who we are so we're mad at the other person. And there begins the destruction of the relationship. Now that's the voice of truth talking!

I give my Dad a big hug and kiss. "Oh I sure am glad to see you Hannah!" My Dad says. "I'm glad to see you Dad, I've missed you so much!" "I'm so proud of you Hannah, you seem to be hanging in there and doing good girl." "Yeah well, I was just sharing with Grandma that the big girl panties are hard to wear some days! I would love to be your little girl again! That was the good life!" He laughs at me. "You always make me laugh Hannah. You have a way of putting things, that always brings a smile. I do miss my little Hannah, it sure was a lot easier to parent little people than you big people. When you were little I could fix most any of your hurts or problems but, I can't now. I just have to love and try and guide you as you go through the course of life. Ain't that a bitch!" We all laugh! I hug my brother David and his wife Jess, and my favorite niece and nephew Zoe and Zach. "Wow it has been to long! Would you look how big you two are!" Zoe says, "we missed you Aunt Hannah, how's comes you lefted us?" I love her sweet little voice. "Well I had to move to where I work." "Why can't you work here?" Well I could but, I wanted to try somewhere new." "Me don't like that Aunt Hannah! Me wants you to come back so we can play!" "Well I'm here now Zoe, so let's play!" What a great time! I am so full I feel like I could pop! I sit there taking in all the sounds and smells.

I take a picture in my heart! I will carry it forever! My Dad sits down and says, "so tell me Hannah, what is the problem?" "What do you mean Dad?" "Come on, I know you Hannah Marie." "Oh Dad, it's my heart and a boy." "Well do you want to tell me about it?" "Yes." So I share the story of Ben, and my Dad says "oh my sweet Hannah, I hate that your heart is hurt but that is part of the deal, finding love." "Well it sucks Dad!" "That is true, it does sometimes."

"I have to go back and I don't know what to do about Ben. I really felt like we had something special and now I just don't know what to think." "Well my sweet girl, I don't know what to tell you when it comes to matters of the heart, nobody can tell you truly what to do." "I know Dad, I just wish somebody could give me an easy answer that would fix it." "Well my dear Hannah, I will pray for you, you seek God and the answer will come to you, that much I know. I know you feel like you're a big girl now but, you still have much to learn my dear." "Don't I know that, Dad!"

David, Jess and the kids leave. Dad says he has to meet Cookie at her son's house for a birthday party. We hug and say goodbye. They all promise to come visit. Sis and I clean Grandma's kitchen and put everything up. "Thank you Grandma! I needed this time with you and family." "Yes it does ground us again to get back to our roots." "I agree!" "Hannah I don't know what will happen for you and Ben but, I know you will be okay!" "I know Grandma." "Now don't you wait so long to come home." "It wasn't my plan, I just could not afford to come." "Well you should have told me, I would have sent you the money." "I know but, I wanted to not have to ask for money." "Oh yes, your big girl panties!" "Yes, and they will wedgie on you!" She laughs! "I'm proud of you Hannah!" "You're the best Grandma! What would I do without you? I never want to know!" Well you won't ever have to know, because whether I'm here or heaven, I will always be in your heart!" "I know that Gram, but I don't like thinking of you not being here!"

Sis has to go and meet Bill, and I'm supposed to meet Ruth and see her family, they're like my second family. I have missed them! I hug my Grandma extra hard! Thinking about all she said to me, I realize we don't know what's down the road, but what we have right in front of us is to be celebrated! I take another picture in my heart of my Grandma. "I always have a hard time leaving you Grandma." "I know you do honey, but Grandma is right in here always," as she puts her hand on my heart. "You are right Grandma, lots of the time when I am having a struggle, I hear your voice reminding me who I am." "Oh that gives me goose bumps to hear. So you know you carry me wherever you go." "Yes I do!" "Me too!" my sis pipes in. "Oh I love you two girls, to heaven and back!" "Back at you Grandma! One more big hug and we are on our way." We go back to Morgan's to get my car. I give Bill a hug, "oh congratulations on getting the best girl in the world!" "I agree," he says! "I'm excited for you two! You're lucky you get me in the deal too!" He laughs! I hug Sis and tell her I'll be back later to stay. "Ok. We should be back by nine, right Bill?" "Yeah, I think so." "Well here Hannah, let me give you a key just in case." "Ok. Have fun see ya later." I head for Ruth's house. She is back at her Mom and Dad's until she can save some money. I pull up in the drive way, and memories of growing up flood my mind. Ruth and I have had some funny times. It's hard being a teenager! I mean, we never ever intended to cause anyone heartache or stress especially our parents but, I guess we did. We just wanted adventure and a good man! Well there was adventure but, the man is still part of our imagination. Good news, Ruth broke up with Jeff! Woohoo!

Knock on the door and Daddy answers, "oh hey Hannah Marie." "Hey Daddy I've missed you!" "We've missed you too! Ruth is in her room." I hear Mama, "hey Hannah Marie, get yourself in here and let Mama see you!" I go in and give Mama a big hug, oh I've missed you girl!" I love the southern ways. I'm never just Hannah, I'm Hannah Marie! Ruth is Ruth-Ann. It's sweet I think. It has always made me feel special. "So tell me, what's going on with you?" So I tell her about my job and all of the Evan drama, and then tell her a little about Ben. "Well it sounds like a good move to The Hair Tamer. You make that boy work for you, and if he is not willing then you move on." "You're right Mama." "I'm so proud of you!" "Thanks Mama!" "Now go talk some sense into Ruth Ann. She broke up with ol'Jeff." "I know she told me. Well I'm glad!" "Me too but, I know it's still hard for her. Well she is better off!" "I agree! I'm gonna go see what she is doing back there." Head back to Ruth's room, and she is on the phone with Jeff. She is crying. She tells Jeff she has to go. I hug her big! "Well aren't we a pair!" "That's no lie," she says. "Let's go to *Vips Big Boy* and have some strawberry pie!" Now he is the man we can depend on to always make us smile with a hot fudge cake or a strawberry pie! Ruth and I would always go to *Vips* when we needed to talk things out, or just sit and make each other laugh and the dessert is wonderful too! "I just pigged out at Grandma's, but you know I will never let you pie alone!" "I love you Hannah, and how I miss us!" "Yeah long distance is hard! Well fix your make up and let's get to the *Big Boy*!"

Ruth and I settle in at the *Big Boy*, they're out of our favorite strawberry pie so we decide on a hot fudge sundae. We will share because I am so full,1 it's crazy that I'm even going to eat more. Ruth needs me, and I need her. She shares her troubles with Jeff, and I try to just listen and not say to much. "You were right Hannah." "What?" I ask her. She smiles, "you were right about Jeff." "I'm sorry that I was because it hurt your heart but, so happy you figured it out before you spent more of your time with him." "It's just hard, you know." "Yes I do!" "He says he is not giving up. I just want him to leave me alone for awhile." "I hope he will," I say to her. "My Mom said to me today that there are lots of fish in the ocean, if you catch the wrong one just throw it back and fish again." Ruth asks, "what if you catch that same fish again? Maybe we should throw it on the bank, and well... you know." "Maybe, I mean we would be saving others from that bad fish!" Laughter. "Oh Hannah, I wish you did not have to go back!" "I know but, I do. I wish you would come visit." "I would like that, but you know I don't have the money and you know how my parents are. No way would they let me take their car, plus go by myself." "True. Maybe when my Mom and Morgan come you could come with them." "Good idea! So your turn, what will you do about Ben?" "Well nothing for now. Ben needs to figure it out, and until he does I'm done." "Wow Hannah, you sound so tough!" "I hope I can stay tough. I just really don't want to waste time on drama, Ruth." "You are grown-up sounding Hannah!"

"You think so?" "Yes I do! You are different since you left town. I can tell, you have grown-up a lot. I think that's what I need to do, get out of this town. But I don't see any light at the end of that tunnel right now." "Don't give up hope, it'll happen Ruth." "Hannah let's make a promise that we won't drift apart, I feel like when people's lives take different directions it seems harder to stay close." "Oh Ruth, we're part of each other and we know too much about each other, we have to stay friends!" We both laugh. "I guess you're right we both we do know too much about each other. But I promise I will always be your best friend." "And you always be my best friend!" We continue to share for another hour, and have laugh 'til our cheeks hurt! I realize it's getting late and I have to get up and get ready and go back to Tall Pines in the morning, so I need to get back to Morgan's. Ruth and I drive back to her house. The house is dark, everyone's in bed so we hug each other hard, reminding each other of our promise. Ruth says, "Hannah I hope you realize you're the glue that keeps us together." I smile at her and say, "you're silly Ruth." "No really, Hannah." "Okay then, you're stuck!" "Please don't ever let me be lost!" "Never." I tell her. "Ok. I love you!" "Love you too Hannah! Mizpah!" "Mizpah!" I watch my friend until she is safe inside, and head for my sister's house. She and Bill are cozy on the couch, watching a movie. So I join them until I can't keep my eyes open. I say goodnight, and lay in bed thinking of what a great day I had with my family! I am glad I came home! So I suppose I can thank Ben and Vicky! *Choosing better, Hannah! That a girl!* Sweet dreams!

I get up, pack my stuff, load my car and back to Tallpines I will go. Sis left for work early, so I am ready to get back home and I don't want to get there late. I do have a lot to do for the week ahead. It just hit me, this is my last week with *the King!* Oh, the lessons learned. I am feeling excited about working at Carla's. I am trying to keep my focus on the left side of my paper, as my Grandma told me to do. I do have so much to be grateful for. I have a lot to share with Juanita. Wonder what advice she will have for me.

Pulling into town, I think how fast that trip went. First stop, the bank to put in my paycheck's. I did shop a little with my sis, so need to make sure I have money to pay for my broken heart shopping club. My sister is a firm believer in retail therapy, and I do believe it helped! I feel stronger after time with my family and I consider Ruth's family to be my family too! I will stop at the grocery store for a few things. I run into Wilma, "oh hey there Hannah!" "Hi Wilma!" "I was thinking and talking to God about you this morning." "Really? What were you talking about?" "You and your Ben." "Well, turns out he is not my Ben." "What are you saying?" "Wilma, he had a girlfriend for two years. And as she puts it, they were on a break. He never even told me about her!" "Oh my dear! Well shit fire, I say!" I laugh to myself! Wilma has a way with words! "Oh I hate to hear that Hannah!" "I know, but oh well I guess it's not meant to be right now." "You're right honey, God's got perfect timing, I know. I am going to keep on believing for you, the right man." "Please do." She hugs me and says, "I've got to skedaddle, my Charlie will be home soon and I have something special planned for him!" "I can only imagine!" "I'll be praying, you can be sure!" "Thanks Wilma! Bye!"

I pull up the driveway and I see Jack run out to the deck hollering my name. "Hannah, Hannah, Hannah! I missed you Hannah!" My heart is overflowing! I run up the deck and grab him in my arms, he holds my cheeks with his little hands and says, "you are the purdiest girl, and I love you Hannah!" "I love you Jack!" So it turns out I do live with the perfect man, he is five years old, his name is JACK! Healing came to my heart through a child! Perfect love casts out fear! I'm grateful to be home!

CHAPTER 10

Closures

Juanita gives me a hug and says, “Ben called. He told me all about what happened.” “Oh did he now.” “I’m sorry Hannah. So what will you do?” “I’m gonna leave him alone, he needs to figure it out and decide where his heart is.” “Yeah I think he knows where his heart is but, he is struggling a little. I think the old girlfriend knows how to work him.” “Well there you go, that is why I’m out for now.” “He asked you to call him tonight. I guess I need to, just for the closure.” “I think so, although I’m not gonna tell you what to do.” “Well I wish you would, nobody wants to tell me what to do on this.” “I don’t think Ben set out to hurt you. He sounded really pitiful.” “Why does that make me happy?” We start laughing, “it feels good to be home, I missed you and Jack! That night, I came home. And wished you were here so I could have a safe feeling I guess. I headed home. I’m glad I went though. Was so good to see everyone.” “I bet it was.” “How was yours and Jack’s trip?” “ It was good, we needed to get out of town. Sometimes it’s just good to go so that when you return, you appreciate the beauty of where you live and the good people you live around.” “I agree we really do live in a great place and the community is special!” “So you have your last week with Evan?” “Yep! “I guess this is a week of closures.” “I guess it is. I’m going to look ahead and not behind!” “That’s good Hannah.” “I feel like God said that to me on my way home. I heard in my spirit. *The only reason to look back Hannah, is to see how far you have come.*” “I like that! I need to listen for that voice.” “I’m glad that doesn’t freak you out when I tell you I hear a voice in my spirit.” “Not at all, it’s cool that you listen to it Hannah. Lots hear, but blow it off thinking that’s crazy!”

Pick up the phone to call Ben, I have a giant knot in my stomach as the phone rings. He picks up. “Hello Ben here, how can I help you?” I feel like throwing up right at this moment. "Hey it's Hannah, Juanita said you called." "I did. I just wanted to tell you how sorry I am and that it was not at all my plan for the night." "Wasn't mine either. So we're even there." "I don't know what to say Hannah?" "Why didn't you tell me about her Ben? Why did you make me find out that way?" "I don't know, I guess I just didn't want you to be freaked out about her." "Really? This is a small town, how did you think we wouldn't find out about each other?" "I just didn't want to deal with it I guess." "Well how did that work out for you? Not so good! I went to your house Ben, and it looks like you two are not finished." "I know I walked out and saw you driving off and I'm sure it looked that way, but Hannah I don't want it to be. I just can't explain Vicky, she's complicated. And we were together for two years, so it's just a little hard to just move forward for her." "Well it seems like the both of you are having a hard time Ben, so I'm just going to bow out and let you two work it out." "Hannah please don't cut me out of your life." "I can't play the game Ben. When you get it straight where your heart is, let me know but for now it is goodbye for me."

"I understand Hannah, I guess I was just hoping that…" "That what, Ben? That I would understand you need to comfort your ex- girlfriend? So sorry but, no I don't. I don't care how complicated she is. Done is done and you're not. You're out of town most of the time anyway, so it should not be that difficult without me on the side." "Come on Hannah!" "Ben I had fun with you, and I wish you well! I think we are finished." "I disagree! You will see me again." "It's a small town so I'm sure I will." "You are my hairdresser!" I have to laugh at that! "Ok. See ya when you need a haircut." "I'm still crazy about you Hannah!" "Stop Ben! I need to get ready for tomorrow, so I better go." "Alright but, can I call you?" "When you can report no more to Vicky. As long as you are still involved in anyway, I can't talk to you. If you were my boyfriend I would not want another girl talking to you." "She is not my girlfriend anymore!" "Well I don't think it's clear to her or you. Figure it out Ben. See ya later!" "Oh you will Hannah! Bye! I'm kissing you through the phone!" Click, I hang up. Oh what in the world! Juanita hears me and says, "I'm telling you, his heart wants you Hannah, but he has a string still attached to Vicky." "Well as long as it's there, I won't be." Juanita looks at me with a grin. "What?" I ask. "Look at you, girl! The Hannah I first met would not have stood up for herself, and been this strong! You have grown my friend! I know it has not been pleasant but, I think your time with Evan has made you a stronger person." "You're right,

I do feel stronger and not so pitiful." "Well Hannah you can either be pitiful or powerful, but you can't be both, and you my friend have stepped over to powerful!"

"I am woman, hear me roar!" "You roar, girl!" We start laughing! "I did feel for Ben a little." "Well time will tell the story." "True, we shall see." To be continued. "I am his hairdresser, he said to me." "Oh how funny! Take his money!" "Oh I will!" We laugh again! Time for bed and Jack wants me to read to him tonight. "It's your turn to read Hannah." "My turn, yeah! I love story time, it's my happy place! He decides on *Green Eggs and Ham* and *Goodnight Moon*. So much fun to read! I go to bed thinking about kissing Ben in the park, and in the dark on a train, and on a plane! Oh Hannah, get over it already! Goodnight moon!

Waking up excited for the day! I will be glad to bring this week to a close. I have to work at the shoe store a half-day so I'll start at the beauty shop, and finish at Shoe Heaven. I love my shoe store job, not because I love shoes but because of Dorothy and Margie. I'm thinking about what Juanita said about me being stronger, and how Ruth said I was different. I think, yes Evan has affected me, but I think of how Dorothy, Margie, Sue, Polly, Rosie, Carla, Wilma, Harold and Evelyn and so many others have changed who I am. Well really, they have all helped me to find who I am. And I know I'm not done yet. There is more of Hannah, I know. I am seeing my reflection in the mirror and I realize I am becoming a beautiful reflection of the people I serve. And who we are, will be a continued work and the Hannah today won't be the Hannah tomorrow. I hear in my spirit, *for He who began a good work is faithful to complete it.* I'm a good work, according to the creator! That is a happy thought! Ok off to work I go.

I walk into work determined to stand in the place of gratitude and I think to myself, be thankful Hannah, for the stepping stone. I say good morning to Evan and he actually says good morning back to me without any negative vibes. Could it be my choice to be grateful that caused the change in him? Hmm I don't know but I'm glad for it, whatever the reason. He asks me to check the towels and get the coffee going. "Okay." I say. Folding the towels and Evan walks in and helps me. It feels kind of awkward. I'm not use to him helping me. I'll take it though. "How was your weekend?" he asks me. Not wanting to share the drama, I said it was good, "I went home for the weekend and it was much needed time with my family." "Good," he says. "Glad you had a good one." I'm really freaked out now! Who is this man and where did *the King* go? "How was your weekend?" I ask. "Good, just got things done and had time on Sunday at Carrie's parents." "Oh that's nice." "Well we had some news to tell them." I'm not sure what to say. "Oh?" I say. "We had to tell them that she is pregnant." "Well congratulations! That's big news!" "Yeah it took me by surprise and still trying to get used to it." "So how did they take the news?" "The first thing they wanted to know is when we would get married." "Well I think that's normal." "Well we are waiting. I don't think you get married for that reason. I mean, we have been having issues and I don't think a baby will fix those." "Maybe not but, they are God's greatest miracle I think." "You have a lot to learn Hannah." "I'm sure I do Evan, but I want to focus on the good." "Ok Pollyanna." he answers.

"However it turns out Evan, I'm happy for you both. I know Carrie will be a great mom." "Yes I agree Carrie will be a great mom." I'm so confused by him this morning. "Well I better go get ready for my first client." "Yeah me too. I bet you're happy this is your last week here." I take a deep breath and say, "you know Evan, I'm really grateful for my time here and I do want to leave on good terms." "Ok." he says. I hold out my hand to shake on our decision and he grabs my hand and we shake on it. "Alrighty then, let's go to work!" What is going on with him? What I hear in my spirit is two words, *love and forgiveness* Hannah, that is what is needed. I answer back, why has he been a jerk the whole time with one moment of being kind of nice? He does not deserve it! I have gone ugly now! The gratitude girl has lost it! Thank goodness Sue is coming in for a quick trim! In she walks. "Good morning Hannah!" "Hey Sue! No Weston today?" "No he is doing man things with Grandpa." "Oh good for him!" We head for the shampoo bowl and the conversation begins. I tell her about the weekend and Evan, and share my frustration! "Sorry Sue don't mean to dump on you, but you always have the right advice for me." "I'm glad you trust me. Well first off Hannah, I believe you stood your ground and that my dear is brave." 'See you always make me feel good Sue! You have turned me into a super hero!" I smile! "Well I think the world sometimes makes us think that being a hero has got to do with doing the big heroic things. When being a hero is really about the daily things in life, and our choices. And that can be in standing our ground or taking ground. Whichever way makes you brave. Do you get what I'm saying?" "I think so." "Hannah, life may not be consistent, but we can be, and that's a choice. You see, we don't have to continue to get beat up by someone in order to love them and forgive them. Sometimes we must move on and love them from a distance. Forgiveness is for you dear. We think it is for the other person, but really Hannah, what they do with it is not our business. It's what it does for us is the biggie!"

"I want you to do something for me. I want you to hold your hand in the tightest fist that you possibly can." "Ok." So I do it, I'm holding it as tight as I can. Then Sue says to me, "okay that is your body in un-forgiveness. Now let it go Hannah. That is your body in forgiveness. Now how do you want to live? In un-forgiveness or forgiveness? What feels better?" "Forgiveness!" "You see your body takes on your emotions, and God never intended us to live tied up in knots and that's what un-forgiveness is, just a big knot. We are vessels of the goodness of God Hannah, and I like to think of it like a garden hose that gets kinked up. Yeah you can still get a little bit out, but if you get the kink or knot out, the flow is powerful! I know I want powerful not a trickle, and I think you do too!" "That is such a good picture for me Sue. You are my hero!" "See there, and I didn't even carry you out of a burning building!" "Well you sort of did. The burning building was me!" She laughs! "I knew you would help me get perspective on it all. I will never forget what you taught me today Sue! I will share that lesson with many." "Well I'm glad I could help you. Thank you for fitting me in on short notice and saving me from getting out the scissors on myself. So you were my hero today!" "Well I always feel like I should pay you Sue, you always make me feel rich after our time together!" "I love my hair! I have got to go, I have a lunch date with my hubby and no kids!" "Oh good for you! See you at the Tamer next time." "Oh yes you will!" We hug and she is out the door. What a great conversation! I need a recorder to help me remember all the great stuff that comes from the beauty shop!

Finish up my beauty shop duties, and head for *Shoe Heaven*. I am sure pleased with the start of my week. Evan said goodbye, he'll see you tomorrow. Miracles in the beauty shop! Walk into *Shoe Heaven* and Margie looks up, smiles and says "I'm glad to see you!" "You, might not be glad to see me." "What?" "I'm sorry I asked off yesterday!" "Oh my dear Hannah I'm sorry, didn't mean to make you worry. We had a huge shipment come in, so we have to get it all put away." "Oh whew! I thought it was bad, like you were going to fire me!" "That will never happen dear. I think you will be quitting us one day when you have too many clients." "I can't think about that! I can't imagine not seeing you every week Margie!" "Thank you Hannah! Now quit puffing up your boss and get to putting up shoes! My heads so big now I might not get out the door!" "Well it's true Margie! You and Dorothy amaze me. I hope to be like you one day." "That is kind, but you are your own amazing, Hannah. Don't forget that!" "Okay, I'm going into Heaven where the shoes live!" We laugh! Well have fun with them. "I will! If they start talking call me!" Funny, and creepy too! "Oh by the way, where is Dorothy?" "Jim felt bad still so she stayed home with him. She said to call her so you all can reschedule your dinner." "Okay." Finished getting the shoes put up just in time. Margie comes in the back and says, "wow I can't believe you got it all done! Good job Hannah! You have been our best employee. I wish you were here everyday!" "Thank you Margie! Now neither one of us will fit out the door tonight for swollen heads!" "Well we are good for each other's self-esteem!" We close up and walk out the door together. Margie has to go pick up her kids. I'm going home to my man, Jack and his Mama! Driving home I think about how life went from devastation to a peaceful feeling. Love and forgiveness, still working on it, but the road there sure is better!

My week of closure went better than I thought it would. I prepared for the worst and hoped for the best! I believe hope won. Evan was the best he has ever been. I guess maybe he got better. I hope so. I finish loading my car with all my beauty shop supplies and walk in one last time to give Evan my keys and a card I got him. Funny thing, I feel a strange sadness. Not one that wishes I were staying but, maybe that it could have been different. Oh well, I give my key over and the card which says, "Evan, I am grateful for the experience here and will carry the lessons with me always. Thank you for the opportunity. I wish you the best. With gratitude, Hannah." I go to shake his hand and feel like I need to give him a hug. So I do. He has a hard time receiving it but does. I walk out the door and wonder, what will he do with the experience? I pray he chooses better. I want to celebrate my new adventure! Going home! I pull in the driveway and there is a couple of cars. Huh, maybe she is having a get together and forgot to tell me. I walk up the deck and open the door and hear, "surprise!" There is Nicole, Katie, Juanita, Shelly, and Carla. My heart takes a picture! My new life, friends and family! Tears roll down my cheeks and they all come over to me and we have a group hug. "You all are the best! Thank you for being here!" Juanita says, "let's get this party started!" "Okay I'm ready!" We eat and drink, and of course we talk! The girl talk is flying! Katie gave Jared the boot and he is begging back. I tell about Ben and we all wonder, what is it? You are nice, and they don't get it. And then you turn ugly, and they are all over you? *What's a girl to do* is our theme tonight! We decide we will meet once a month at a different house and have a girl night and give it a theme. This girl is loving her life! Even though I miss Ben. Yes the voice of truth!

CHAPTER 11

Born for This

I'm settled in at *The Hair Tamer*, I love my new space and I love working with Carla. And soon we will have a new hairdresser working with us, her name is Susie. She is a tiny girl that loves her makeup. Wilma is going to love her style! Only negative is, Vicky is across the street. So I feel watched. I have been dating and still have not found the one that gives me that feeling Ben did. Carla said I need to quit comparing. I'm trying. I feel like I'm always trying something. My business has grown and I think soon I will have to quit Shoe Heaven. I am working late nights at the shop to fit everyone in, so I can work with Dorothy and Margie. Jim has been really sick so I want to be there for Dorothy, and staying at the shoe store helps her I think. I have not talked to Ruth for awhile. She is busy and has a new group of friends, and I'm busy too. I have called but missed her. I think about her saying, I'm the glue that holds us together. I'm trying Ruth! I do miss her! Nicole and I have really become close, which is hard because of Josh and Ben. I think no matter what, we will always be friends. She gets me, and we have the same sense of humor. Her and Josh struggle because of his jealousy. Funny, I don't think Ben has that. Although I did not have a lot of time with him, I never felt that from him. He has been out of town working a lot. He called for a haircut, but then had to cancel because of work. The beauty shop continues to teach me and I realize I was made for this. I read just the other day a quote by Mark Twain "The two most important days of your life: the day your were born and the day you realize why you were born." I find people fascinating but, at times they can be stressful. Me included. I know I am suppose to love and encourage people and make them feel beautiful. It's more than their hair, it's about having a safe place, feeling cared for and relaxed.

So that is what I want, to provide a safe place for people to feel cared for and loved.

Carla and I clear out a place for Susie to put her supplies. It will be good to have another person here. Carla is so busy and then add her husband and kids to the mix? The girl never stops! I wonder how I will handle the load when, and if I marry and have a family. I hope as good as Carla! I have a new summer time client coming in. I stop to sit for a moment and rest. It has been one of those days. I have not even had time to go to the rest room, let alone have lunch. Oh well, I'm just happy to sit for a minute. The door opens and in walks a women I don't know. I ask, "can I help you?" "Yes" she says. "I need my hair done." "Okay, when were you thinking?" "Now!" "Well I don't have time right now." "Well maybe if you got off your ass you would!" I kind of laugh, thinking she is joking. She is not! "Ma'am I just sat down, I'm waiting for my next customer to walk in." "Oh really? she says, as if I'm lying to her. She then tells me I am not going to be a success with my attitude being in a service job. I say, "what are you talking about ma'am? I have not stopped all day and I just sat down because I have a client coming in any minute, and you walk in and announce that you need your hair done right this moment? I'm sorry I don't have time." "You can make time!" "Well when I figure that one out I will be a billionaire so I won't be doing hair." "Oh and you're a smart ass too!" *Ok Hannah, breathe!* "I do not have time for you, I'm sorry!" She gets in my face and points the Mother finger at me and says, "you listen, I'm gonna remember this and tell everyone I know about you!" "I will remember you, and tell everyone *I* know, how not to treat another person. Oh and Ma'am if I did have time, it would not be for you, ever!"

She storms out and slams the door. I'm just sitting there thinking, what in the world just happened? Who was that woman? I think I just saw the devil! So she just told me I'm a lazy ass, and a smart ass! I guess that's what you call assuming. Makes an ass out of me and you, there you go! I laughed to myself thinking I just wanted a place where people could come in and feel loved, safe and rest. Then that happens. Oh, people do work on our holiness! I tried to stay calm but, she got me in the end. What is with bullies? I know my Grandma would say it's about them. I think there is just going to be some mean people in life. I hear my Grandma say, *so step over them and move on girl.* That is right, I'm not going to let her ruin my day. I just hope my next customer is a nicer, kinder person than that one that just left!

In walks Mable, she is a cute little lady with an English-accent. I introduce myself and she hands me a bag. She says, "I brought lunch for you, because I know you are not having one today." "That is so kind of you." "Well it was kind of you to fit me in today." She needs a shampoo set, "so I will eat when I put you under the dryer." I tell her. She begins to share her story, she is from Scotland so that is her accent. She was a war-bride. Her husband and her, sold everything and bought a motor home. They have been traveling the States for the past year. "That sound amazing!" "Well it has been, but to be quite honest with you, I don't like not having home base." "Yes I guess I never thought about that." "Well I thought I did but turns out I didn't realize how much I would miss having a home. Now my hubby is quite content with it. So we shall see we're trying to decide. He said he wants me to be happy, so whatever I want he will be happy to do, although he has enjoyed not having all the work and care of the home." Mabel has the most beautiful green eyes and the prettiest silver hair I've ever seen. I would love to see a picture of her in her younger years. She says they are loving this area and may look at some homes around here. "Oh good." I tell her, "I would love more time to get to know you better." "As would I, you Hannah." I finish rolling her up and thank her for lunch.

"Now off to the dryer with you, miss Mabel." It's kind of nice. I'm sitting here eating the turkey sandwich and chips, Mabel brought me and enjoying the peace. Carla had to leave early today, her daughter had a volleyball game in another town. She's a beautiful girl, Carla has been coloring her hair since she was five, it just cracks me up. Carla said to me, "my mom said 'now you got your own live doll,' I guess she use to cut and color her baby doll's hair. Her mother said it was no surprise to her that Carla would be a hairdresser. We are all wired for something and maybe a few things. Ruth comes to mind again. Wonder what she will end up doing? She is still searching for her purpose. Funny how some find theirs right away, and some search for awhile till they find theirs. Oh, the dryer clicked off and miss Mable is fast asleep. I touch her leg and she wakes. "Oh my, I fell asleep." "Yes the dryer has that effect on most. I love to get under one in the winter. They are like a sleeping drug." "Well I agree. I don't think I ever stay awake under one." I get her combed out and she is pleased with what she sees in the mirror. "You did a fabulous job Hannah! Can I make an appointment for next week?" "You sure can!" We get her set, and I thank her for the lunch again. "You make the best sandwich!" "My hubby says that too. Glad you enjoyed it." "I had the meanest lady come in before you so you were like sunshine after a ugly storm!" "Oh my, what in the world?"

"That's what I said. I will tell you about it next week." "Ok I will remind you. You have got me curious."

"Have a good week Mabel, and if I hear of any houses I'll let you know. Oh please Hannah, do let me know, it's said that you can find out everything in the beauty shop." "You know there is a bit of truth to that Mabel, there's a lot of things that are talked about in the beauty shop. Some are quite shocking!" "Oh believe me, I've heard my share. I've spent a few hours in the beauty shop myself." We both laugh! "Well it makes for a good story later, doesn't it Mabel?" "That it does Hannah!"

I'm winding down my day waiting on my last client, It's Shelly. She works at Don Juan's, the best Mexican food you've ever eaten, and they have the best tacos! We have become friends. She is always trying new things. I love that about her. She is running late. I see her pull up. I open the door, "hey there!" "Oh I'm so sorry I'm late Hannah!" "It's ok." "No it really is not. Your time is valuable." "Well I know you didn't do it on purpose." "No but, I think sometimes people don't realize what stress they cause you guys when we come late. It messes up your day." "Well you're my last one so we are good. What do you want to do with your hair?" She whips out a picture. "Okay Shelly, I'm gonna give it to you straight. This girl has a lot of hair, and plus they have a fan on her blowing it back like that." She starts laughing! "You can't blame a girl for dreaming, can you?" I laugh too! "No that is one of my favorite things about you. We can cut it into that shape, but you will have to style it different." "Well let's give it a try. Oh Hannah, did I tell you I'm taking a stained glass class?" "No. I love stain glass!" "Why don't you do it with me?" "I don't know if I would be good at it." "Well who knows 'til they try. I mean, you didn't know if you could do hair 'til you tried, right?" "Right." "Ok then, I will sign you up." "Wait I need to find out when it is." "It's Wednesday nights at seven." "I think I can do that. It makes me nervous." "Good that means you should do it! In order to grow Hannah, we must step out of our comfort zones!" "I know, you're right! I guess that is why God put you in my life Shelly, to get me out of my comfort zone!" "Oh I thought it was to give you your best taco experience!" "That too!" "So you still seeing Jake?" "Yes." "What about Ben?" "No he has not been around. I like Jake, he just isn't Ben." "Well here's a saying my Mom had on our wall growing up. *If you love something set it free. If it comes back to you, it's yours. If it doesn't, then it never was.*" "I know I just wish I could get over him!" "I get it girl! It's tough stuff. Time is all I can say." I finish her hair and it looks even better than I thought it would. She loves it! "I will call you next week, and if you want I'll come get you for class." "Sounds good!" We hug and she waits on me to close so I don't leave alone. "Good night!" "Night! Love my hair like always!" "I'm glad!"

CHAPTER 12

More People "Lois"

"Lois? She owns *Red's* bar… the older crowd gathers there." I said that in front of Carla. She said, "who you calling old, girl?" "Well I mean, there are no people my age that go to *Red's*." Lois is the kindest woman. She looks just like the witch in *Wizard of Oz*, the bad one so it's quite confusing when you look at her because you think of the bad witch, but she really is the good witch. Well, I mean she has the personality and the kindness of the good witch. She takes care of several people. She has no children of her own. She takes care of her niece and nephew. Although they are grownups now, she still takes care of them financially. Carla says she's quite wealthy but you would never suspect it. She dresses very plain and is very humble. Really I don't know why I'm saying that, not all people with money are fancy dressers. But also, she drives an old LTD. Carla said she could drive any car she wanted, but she's just content with her life and living it simple. She said when she finds something she likes, she sticks with it. That's why she didn't get married she said. She never found a man she wanted to stick with. She also takes care of an older woman, Connie Sue. I thought Connie Sue was her mother for a while, but then found out that she was just an old friend that has worked for her and had no one to care for her, so Lois took her on and cares for her just like she was her mother. You would never pick Lois as someone that owns a bar. I mean, she's very quiet and reserved. I don't know, I just always thought of the bar owner as being somebody kind of loud and boisterous. What do I know? Once again, don't judge Hannah. So while Lois is living simply, her niece built the big beautiful home, drives a Cadillac, and Pete her nephew, well poor guy he's the town drunk. Nice as he can be, but always drunk. Sad. So Lois is a guardian angel for many.

CHAPTER 13

More People "Connie Sue"

Connie Sue, she's a hoot! She's about three foot-two and has some sort of arthritis where her back is hunched over, so she looks as if she's looking at the ground all the time. She said everybody teases her and always says to her, "what are you looking for Connie Sue? Did you lose something?" I will say it is a trick to shampoo her and not get water everywhere. She's also on oxygen full-time. She was a heavy smoker she told me, "don't ever do that Hannah, this is what happens and you don't want this." The first time I did Connie Sue's hair, I was scared to death. She wheezes the whole time and sounds like she's taking her last breath. I feel bad for her, that's got to be a scary feeling not to be able to breathe right. She loves the *National Enquirer* magazine, and every time she comes she's cut some kind of article out, this week it was the world's first pregnant boy. She makes me post it up on my mirror for everybody to see, she said the world has got to know about this, it's gone crazy! The sad thing is it's a little starving child from Africa with the swollen belly, but she doesn't realize that. I'm not going to be the one to tell her, so I just go along with her and post it up and tell her "yes the world's gone crazy Connie Sue, what's next?" She always tells me she doesn't know what she would do without Lois. "Lois is my angel," she says. She was unable to have children. "I don't know, I guess the good Lord knows better than I do. Maybe I would not have been a good mother, anyhow he gave me Lois I'm grateful for that." Connie Sue has Snow White hair, and has me brush it a hundred strokes before we wash it . She thinks that keeps it growing and healthy. "I believe it does," I tell her. She is here every Thursday, rain or shine. She said to me one time, "Hannah there are three things I'm sure of." I said, "what is that Connie Sue?" "My hair on Thursday, death and taxes." "That's true Connie Sue." We laugh. I must confess, I pray every time she comes that she will not die at the beauty shop. So far so good.

CHAPTER 14

Pete

Poor ol'Pete, what a sad man. I'm not sure when or if he is ever sober. I have not seen him when he is not drunk. He is a nice looking man except for the wear and tear of being an alcoholic. I'm not sure what happened to his parents and how Lois started caring for him and his sister. Pete has never married. I get that! I think he is in his early forties. That's what Carla thought too. So today I get to cut his hair. Carla usually cuts it but, she didn't have time so I'm it. He should be here by now, I look out the window and I see him weaving as he walks to the shop. Oh no, he is really drunk today! I'm the only one here so I hope it goes well. I'm not afraid of him but, I have not seen him this drunk before. The door opens and a very drunk Pete stands before me. He is doing a balancing act as he mumbles, "here for a haircut." "I'm cutting it today Pete, follow me." He trips and slams into the wall. It's going to be a rough one I think. I give him a little help with his balance, and he is in the chair! I am not even going to try to shampoo him. I just take the spray bottle to him, and hope the cold water will sober him up a little bit. Wishful thinking I'm afraid. I finish wetting his hair turn to get my scissors, turn back and he is past out cold. I try waking him, no response, not sure what to do so I start to try and cut his hair. He's like a rag doll. I tilt his head back, then to the right side and then the left side and forward still no response. He is breathing, so that's good. I can't believe this! They sure don't prepare you for these things in beauty school. When I hold his head up straight he doesn't look too bad I actually did pretty good. I guess all those haircuts I gave my baby dolls when I was a little girl, was training I did not realize I would use. I try again to get Pete to respond, he is just out cold! I hate to call Lois, but somebody's got to come and get him. I call her and she says, "oh I'm so sorry honey, I'll send someone right away." Lois pulls up in her LTD, she and a man I don't know get out. I will never forget the look on her face. It hurt my heart. The man with her was a big man, and he just grabbed Pete up. Lois smiled and looked at me and said, "Hannah I have no idea how you manage to get his haircut, and it looks good." "Thank you Lois." "No thank you! If he ever shows up like that again, you don't mess with him. You call me and I'll come get him." "I wasn't sure what to do." "Well that's a haircut you will remember." "Yes Ma'am!" I say. "Oh I need to pay you, here you go honey." She sticks a one hundred dollar bill in my hand. "I will get you change." "Oh no you won't." "Lois that is too much." "Hannah what you just put up with, is worth that and more! You take that!" "Well thank you so much!" "You're welcome, and sorry for the trouble." "Good night Lois." "Good night."

CHAPTER 15

It's *All About Me* (Lessons From A Narcissist)

So I looked up narcissist in the dictionary, it says "a person who has an excessive interest in, or admiration of themselves. Narcissists think the world revolves around them."

• • •

I told Carla that Kathy was coming to me for color, and she said good luck. "She is the hardest person to please. I don't care what you do it will never be right, but she'll come back just so she can tell you that you don't know how to do it, and she knows better than you do. Let me tell you what happened and why Kathy quit coming to me." "Oh I'd love to hear the story." "Well she made an appointment for highlights, so I had three hours booked because you know she has a ton of hair." "Yes she does." "So she forgets her appointment. So we reschedule her and book her again for three hours. She stands me up again." "Oh my gosh!" "It gets better, I call her and say, 'Kathy this is Carla, you didn't come for your appointment.' So long story short we book her again, and again she forgets. So this time I call and she says, 'oh my goodness I guess I forgot, it slipped my mind. When can you get me in? I need it as soon as possible I look a mess!' No sorry or apology of any kind." "Wow! Then what?" "I tell her, Kathy I'm going to need a credit card to reschedule you. 'What are you talking about Carla? I am not giving you a credit card to reschedule me, if that's the case I will find someone else to do my hair.' Kathy you have missed three 3 hour appointments and every time you do that, it costs me time and money that I don't have. 'Well you listen to me Carla, I run a business and I have two kids and a husband so excuse me if I forget!' Kathy, I run a business and have a husband and two kids so I get it but, you work by appointments right? You're a realtor, you have appointments to show property and I work by appointment too, so I have to keep an appointment book to keep things straight. We all make mistakes but, I can't keep booking out three hours and have nothing to show for it. It's business and your a business person so I hope you understand. Well she didn't, so she quit coming to me. I have a customer that used to work for her and she said she is the queen of making rules that no one else can break, but she can break them all the time and never apologize. But, it's okay because she is the only one that has life happening to her. I hope you have a better experience Hannah."

• • •

So my experience was no different with Kathy and a few others, but I came to understand who and what a narcissist is about. She has let ego be her master, and all the ego wants is reward. She can't get no satisfaction! What a sad life to live, having a beautiful garden and only seeing the weeds of disappointment. She hungers for the goodness in life, but eats the seeds and never plants them, all the while blaming all around her for the lack of fruit in her garden. I'm having a flashback of a revival that Ruth's mom sent us to one time, and the preacher said, "you know these people, they have troubles with their I's. *I'm this, I'm that. I, I, I, me, me, me!* They never consider how life affects anyone but themselves." What a sad story!

CHAPTER 16

Life keeps on Teaching and so do People

So it's another day at the office. We are all busy doing our thing. Susie is doing well and has a new man. He had a motorcycle accident and lost a leg. But seems to function well with his prosthetic leg. You can hardly tell. He is good looking and seems nice. We are in the break room talking and Susie says to Carla, "and you know the saying, when God takes away he gives back double?" "Yeah," we answer. "Well I know where that is on Kevin!" Her eyes wide as she says it! "Things got hot with us last night and, well you know. When I saw it, I asked him if we could just talk." Carla and I break into laughter! "So did you have a good talk?" "Yeah, he was so sweet. After the talk we decided to wait on making love. I have to be honest, I'm scared!' Carla says, "oh great, now our eyes will want to look straight at his crotch." We all laugh! "But really, it is concerning! I am crazy about him!" "So if he is the right one, he will wait for you Susie." "Yeah you're right." "I have to get my lady out of the dryer," Carla says. "And I do too."

• • •

I finish up with Mabel and in walks Sheila, I sit her down in my chair and begin looking at her hair. I notice it is broken off in the back pretty bad! It's like a baby when they have that hair that is broken off from wallowing in bed. So I say to her, "Shelia you have a lot of broken hair in the back here and I don't know why? But I want to show you, so you know I didn't do it." I show her and she says, "oh it's probably from f**king." I kind of laugh, and say "no really." And she says, "really, I love f**king! I f**k a lot!" I'm so not prepared and I look over at Carla, and sweet little Betty who teaches a *Bible* study and never says a bad word. I'm thinking, please stop saying the F word! So I say, "well maybe try a silk pillow case." She says, "well if

I'm f**king at home, I guess that would work but I don't always f**k at home." "Okay well let's do our best to get it fixed, and I think you need a conditioning treatment." I get her conditioned, cut and styled and out the door. "Whew!" Carla says, "wow that was f**king crazy!" We both burst out laughing! She gets Betty out from under the dryer and I say to her, "Betty I am so sorry for my customer's foul language!" Betty said, "oh honey don't you worry about it, it is not your fault. You know I was thinking under the dryer, in all my years I have never known someone that f**ked their hair off!" We all laugh, and once again I judged wrong. Betty could handle it, and even say it! I realize I can't be responsible for how people handle life, nor can I control what they do. I can only run my race! Thank you voice of truth.

CHAPTER 17

Stay *Grateful*

I'm having dinner with Dorothy tonight. Jim is still struggling with his health. Dorothy takes such good care of Jim. Well, they take good care of each other. Jim was in for a haircut last week and I asked him how long he had been putting up with Dorothy, and his answer was, "not near long enough!" I love that! They are both amazing! It has been hard but they stay positive and grateful. Dorothy says, you can always find something to be grateful for.

• • •

I have a busy day today! That makes me grateful! I have two new people today. I still get nervous. Hoping to please them and make them happy. In walks Margret, she has fire red hair and a sweet smile. "Hello I'm Hannah, nice to meet you Margret." "Same here." she says. "I have heard so many good things about you." "I always like hearing that!" So I sit her down and ask her what she wants and she says, "well Hannah, today won't be what I want, but rather what I need." "Ok. What do you need?" "Well I have cancer and I am doing chemo." "Oh my, Margret I'm so sorry!" "Well me too, but it is what it is. So I need you to shave my head. I asked my husband to, but he could not do it. Margie gave me your card and told me Hannah is the best, she will do it for you, so here I am. We have not been here long so I have not got a hairdresser. Sorry our first appointment has to be for this, and I don't know how long before I'll be back." "I'm going to believe for the best!" "Thank you Hannah!" "Well lets do this." I finish buzzing her hair and my heart hurts for this woman I don't even know. She is the first person I have known with cancer. I tell her she looks great with a buzz. "Well it certainly will be easy. I want to find the good!" "That's a positive!" "What do I owe you?" "To get better and come back to me." "Oh no Hannah, let me pay you." "No please let me do this for you." "Ok but, here is a tip." "No please!" "Ok then I will be back!" "I will keep you in my prayers." "Thank You Hannah! I can not tell you how much easier you made this experience!" "I hope so." "You know, we moved from LA, and at times you just feel as if you died in the street, people would just step over you. Don't get me wrong, there are many good people there, it is just the crowdedness and pace there. So although I miss some conveniences, I am enjoying the slower pace of Tall Pines, and oh the fresh air! I will have to travel for treatments, so it will be nice to come home to recover." "Well anything I can do for you Margret please let me know. This is a great community even though small when there is a problem the people come together no matter the differences to help." "That is what I have found in my short time here. So glad I chose to come to you. You have made me feel cared for!" "Well that makes my heart happy!" I hug her and off she goes. I ask God to give her strength and comfort for this, and to kick cancers butt! I smile thinking of what Ruth would say about my prayer. She would probably say, "Hannah should you say butt to God?" I think so! He's God and already knows my thoughts, so why lie? That's where we the people get it wrong I think. Instead of being honest, we play church and act as if we have it all together. I saw something that I cant remember where I saw it, that said *being a Christian does not mean I'm perfect, but that I'm in need of a savior*. I like that! Sometimes at church I just want to yell out, can we just get real! God can handle it I'm sure! I need to call Ruth, I miss her. We have drifted apart for now, but I know we will always love each other. Like she says, "we know too much about one another." Talk about getting real.

• • •

The day flies by, and in walks my next customer. She has a portable music player with her. Carla, Susie and I look at each other. "Hello!" she says, "I'm Tammy. I have a perm with Hannah." "Hello I'm Hannah." Let's just say I was not ready for Tammy! None of us were! "Where can I get this plugged in?" she asks. I point to an outlet. Ok. She's plugged in. She hushes everyone and tells us to listen! "I don't know if you all have heard the Statler Brothers?" I say no, but Carla has. Susie and her customer have not. Well we would all hear them for the next two hours, over and over! If anyone talked, she would hush us and hit rewind and play what she thought we missed over again. She had Carla turn off the shop radio. I can't believe this woman, who none of us knows has taken over the shop, and we are being held hostages by her and the Statler Brothers! That was the longest two hours of my life! Crazy thing is, no one has heard of her and we have no idea where she came from. We were not allowed to talk or ask questions. She was the only one talking, and it was to just give us information on the Statler Brothers. I now know more than I ever wanted to about them! She left and Carla's customer said, "oh my she is a sandwich short of a picnic!" We laugh at that comment. I have never heard that one, it's a good one! Sometimes you have to laugh at life, but it was sad and scary at the same time. Makes you think of how fans can become so obsessed and end up doing crazy things. I'm going to let that go for now. Another thing school can't teach.

• • •

I am finished for the day, so I freshen up to go and meet Dorothy for dinner. We are meeting at Lilly's and it is my treat tonight! I'm so excited about that! I remember my first time at Lilly's, Dorothy treated me. I did not have two dimes to rub together, as my Grandma says. She has the funniest sayings! Dorothy said to me that night I would have my turn one day to treat. This is my day! I look at myself in the mirror and think of what Wilma taught me to do. I say, "I am Hannah Marie Kinsell, a beautiful child of God! Thank you God for the opportunities you have given me and the ones to come!" I feel God smile!

• • •

I get to *Lilly's*. Walk in, and get our table. Here comes Dorothy. I love her! She walks in and you feel the atmosphere change! I want that! I stand up and give her a big hug! "You're the best hugger, Hannah! I always look forward to a Hannah hug!" "Well I always look forward to my time with you Dorothy! I always feel better and richer every time I'm with you!" "We are each other's best fans!" "Yes we are! Speaking of fans," I share Tammy's story with her. "Oh my, she sounds like she needs some help." "I think so." "Well let's pray and believe for her to get that." "Dorothy I so want to be like you, were you always this way? I mean I see some people live their lives rich in some areas, but then not in others. What is the secret?" "Oh Hannah, it's gratitude. I feel like I try to choose to be grateful. I think the big thing we miss Hannah, is God said to be grateful in all things. To enter His gates with thanksgiving. He did not say only when things are perfect, and the way you think they should be give thanks. The Lord's Prayer says, *as it is in heaven so it is on earth*. So I believe it is in that place of thanksgiving or gratefulness, that Heaven is felt on earth. You see Hannah when your heart is filled with gratitude it can't help, but spill out on everyone else! We live from a place of overflow, but few choose to live that way. Most hold tightly to the cup the world has given them, and only let themselves have a small drink every day. Fear keeps them in a prison that most don't even know they are in. It's sad when you know the truth and share it, but people will not receive it. Know the truth and it will set you free!" "Hey that's a Jesus quote." "Yes it is Hannah. Well to make it simple it's the old saying you can take a horse to water but, you can't make him or her drink. People will believe what the world says, so few will walk on the water because the world says you can't! Yes people will make fun of you at times they did Jesus. He could not heal or do miracles in his own town because they did not believe, Hannah." "That's true I never thought about that Dorothy." "Well my dear it's like Glenda the good witch in the *Wizard of Oz*. She said to Dorothy, *you had the power all along my dear*. She had to use it. We have all been given the keys to the kingdom Hannah. You must choose. Even God can't move the parked car, we have to be willing to move. He gave us freedom to choose. It amazes me how many people miss *John 10:10* in the *Bible*." "What is J*ohn 10:10* Dorothy?" "*He came so that we would have life and not just life but life abundant*." "That's awesome!" "Yes it is, but, you will have to battle your mind, because the world and even religion will try to confuse you with different thoughts. God is love and God is good Hannah, and that is all that he can ever be. Abundant life is not just a bank account, it's your spiritual life, your relationships, your health and it's peace and joy. Church should be daily and how we do business and treat our fellow man. People should feel increase and gratitude from us. Love should be who we are as children of God." "That is so good Dorothy! You should be a preacher!" "I don't know about that, I know that I am supposed to share the truth and love people." "I feel like I have more understanding of who God is and who I am in him after listening to what you just said. I feel like religion makes it confusing and truthfully makes God seem mean and angry at times." "Well my dear, that is Man wanting to control. We have to watch out for ourselves, not to become full of ourselves. That leads us to want to rule over people and make them feel beneath us. That is never good! As many people as God gives us to help we can hurt if not led in love. One more thing Hannah, is to be choosy of who we spend the majority of our time with. The *Bible* says, not to give your pearls to the swine. In loving people and not wanting to be disappointing, we sometimes will do things that we are not called to do. You see Hannah, lots of things will call to you, but make sure they're for you. Just because it's a good thing or a good person, does not mean it's for you. I pray you learn that one quicker than I did." "Do you think, Dorothy? I mean, look how long I stayed at Evan's." "Yes but, you mustn't beat yourself up over that Hannah. You're young and learning truths that are hard, especially when people choose to be less, and try to blame you for their issues. Good news, you have grown from it and become better for the experience." "Yes that's right Dorothy!" "You see how your mind and thoughts can play tricks with you? You can take two approaches Hannah, to find the good in what happened, and be grateful for the lesson, yes dear, even the bad, or you can beat yourself up instead and become the victim person, we have talked about. It's all about what you choose to think who's thought you want to think about." "Well Dorothy, I call it the voice of truth. Since I was a little girl I could hear a voice inside of me that would always make me feel happy and peaceful, like I was okay, no matter what! I always felt it was Gods voice. So religion was confusing to me, because it was rare that, that voice and the voice of religion were the same." "Oh Hannah, do I understand!" "I'm so glad. I have never share that with anyone 'til now." "Well I feel honored that you would trust me to share your beliefs and heart with." "I do Dorothy! Thank you for your belief in me, even when I don't have it for myself. Never have you ever made me feel bad or weird about me!" "Well I'm glad about that! I would never ever want to do that to you or anybody. So in a nutshell my dear Hannah, live grateful and always look for how God will turn things to good for you, because he will my dear. That I know. The one last thing, is to renew your mind. God says, it's by the renewing of our minds. So seek truth! The game changers like Edison, the Wright brothers and so many others lived in possibilities. While many made fun and mocked them, they continued to believe in what God planted in them. I love what Edison said, 'I have not failed. I've just found 10,000 ways that it won't work. One more I love.' Opportunity is missed by most people because it is dressed in overalls, and looks like work. Study people that intrigue you and encourage you to dream big to not see impossible but possible! Spend your time renewing your mind in those areas. You see Hannah, as a child of God all things are possible for those who believe! Use your keys!" "I will Dorothy!"

Let's eat! Dorothy blesses our food, and we enjoy our filet mignon. We finish up and I walk Dorothy to her car, hug her and thank her for another wonderful evening and more golden nuggets. "I love our time together

Hannah, and I love that you are always willing to be taught." Give Jim a big hug, tell him I missed him." "Oh you can count on that, I love every opportunity I get to hug my husband. I'll see you next week for my hair dear! Can't wait! Oh and Hannah, thank you so much for dinner tonight dear. I told you that you would treat one day." "Yes you did Dorothy, thanks for your belief in me!"

CHAPTER 18

Keep Loving (Five Years Later)

I can't believe I have been doing hair for six years. Lots of things have changed, and some things have not. I have lost some customers. That has been something that school did not teach. Also I have gained some new customers. I guess I didn't realize how much I would love *my people*, as I call them. This business messes with you in so many ways. You think they are happy and then they never call back and you wonder, what happened? Then you run into them and it can feel awkward. There are times you just want to check on them and you don't, because you don't want to make them feel like you're trying to get them to come back to you. The thing is, you miss them. I also have lost a couple of them to death, Connie Sue and Polly. I am happy Polly is with Pete now, and Connie Sue can breath. But every Thursday I miss Connie Sue, and on Tuesday's, Polly and Rosie. Rosie moved away to live with her youngest daughter after losing her husband Jerry, and sister Polly. Her older daughter broke her heart, and never tried to fix it. I got a card from Rosie the other day and it made me see that sometimes we don't realize, how in our small ways we can make a big difference. Her card said, "My Dear Hannah, you will never know how much you mean to me. You helped me and were a safe place for me to share my heart. I miss our time together. I wish my older daughter had your kind heart. You have been a daughter, friend, confidant and the best hairdresser I have ever had! Please if your ever in my neck of the woods, come and see me. You always have a bed at my house. I hope you are doing good and love has found you! God bless you Hannah. Love, Rosie." Aw, sweet Rosie! My cup runs over! I think back on a conversation with Sue years ago about heroes. "We are saving each other in different ways daily. Our life song should sing of Gods love and being his hands and feet." *I want to keep loving and being grateful.* Oh, voice of truth!

• • •

About loving, Nicole and Josh are married and expecting a baby. I hope on my birthday! My sis is married, and had a huge wedding! Yes, Mother got to her. Bill loved it of course, he loves a party. It was fun! Just not sure my sis loved it, she always puts her happy face on, but I know her, it makes me sad for her. I mean, your wedding day should be your best day! Not sure that hers was. Ruth is married and has moved to Ohio? Although we haven't really hung around each other in a very long time, she asked me to be in her wedding. I'm not sure about the guy she married, I don't think he's the best for her. Not my place to judge that! Mama was in question of him because he has no middle name. She gave him one. "That ain't right Hannah-Marie." she said. Oh sweet Mama! I do love her! Love has found me and his name is Ben! So as Shelly said to me, let love go and if it comes back it's yours. Ben is mine! No more Vicky! She moved away. It was so worth the wait. We are now planning our wedding! I am in my own house now. Talk about big girl panties! Juanita is remarried to Mick, and Jack is getting so big! He still has a huge piece of my heart, which Ben is okay with! Jack is now aware of girls his own age, he said to me, "I always love you Hannah but, I really like a girl named Mia in my class. It 's like, you really like Ben!" "That's right Jack!" We have a date once a week for ice cream and to talk about stuff. I miss our home together, but I am learning there are seasons in life. Change is a sure thing. I finally had to give up my shoe store job. Dorothy and Margie are now my customers! Evan moved away. Carrie and him had a beautiful little girl they named Marie. I asked him if he named her after me. He laughed! I heard he and Carrie have split but, who knows? Not everything you hear in the beauty shop is true! I still love my job!

CHAPTER 19

Time Flies (Five Years Later)

Talk about things changing. Most of my shampoo set ladies I have, are now having their hair blow dried and done with the curling iron. One thing hasn't changed, Wilma's hair! She still touches heaven! She loves that Ben and I are together, and always takes credit for her prayer to find me love. And I will always be grateful for her prayer. Of course she continues to educate me on keeping my marriage spicy. Ben loves it! We have so many good examples for marriage, Jim and Dorothy, Harold and Evelyn. In fact just the other day Ben and I had a disagreement and I had Evelyn that morning. She asked me, what's wrong Hannah? You're not yourself. So I began to share my frustrations about Ben. She listened very patiently. When I finished she said to me, "you know Hannah, many years ago I went to a woman's retreat weekend. I was feeling a little frustrated with Harold at that time and was very discontent. What I walked away with that weekend was this, if I was always looking at what Harold wasn't, I would never see what Harold was. You see my dear, I'm not telling you that you can't be disappointed at times in one another, but if we're always looking for what each isn't, we miss out on so much more. What each other are!" "You are so right Evelyn, I'm sorry this is your time and I'm spending it whining." "Don't you ever be sorry Hannah, this was a divine appointment. We all have our moments in life when it feels big and overwhelming. God sends us a messenger at just the right time if we pay attention. Today I'm your messenger! Tomorrow you may be mine." "You're right Evelyn! Thank you for being mine today. You know, as I think about what you just shared with me, I realize that can be in all relationships. I think about a scripture in the *Bible* that says, *what you seek you will find.*" "Yes Hannah, that is true! If you look for disappointment you usually will find it, if you look for beauty you will find it. There is also a scripture that says, *love holds no record of wrongs*. That is one thing we all must work on, is letting go of offense. When you keep a list of wrongs, you become a self-righteous person, full of judgment. And that road my dear, leads to a sad lonely life. Who wants to be around a person you feel is keeping watch over ever little thing you do wrong You see Hannah, none of us are perfect so we could all keep a list if we wanted. It's about forgiveness. Which we all need." "True, I don't want to be that person that keep a list of wrongs. What a great message Evelyn." I finish her hair and off she goes. The voice of truth.

• • •

Another thing that has happened, Carla has moved and I bought her shop. Yes, I am the owner of *The Hair Tamer*! A friend of mine from beauty school has moved to Tall Pines and is working with me. Alice is awesome and has really great ideas! So Susie and I are grateful to have her. We miss Carla! I am so grateful and always will be for her love and care over me. She was the best boss ever! I hope to follow her lead. The best news is Ben and I have a two-year old son, Myles. What a joy he is, and Ben is the best Dad! We have managed to find a way to work out his out-of-town time. We call it "mini vacation time." We meet up and it's our special time. We also have another baby on the way. Katie keeps Myles when I work, and has three kids of her own. It's hard to leave him, thank God for Katie and her love for him and me. He enjoys her kids and they are sweet with him! Katie and Jake made it. He got Jesus, and is a total different man. He quit drinking too, that helped. I was worried about how things would go having Myles, and having to work but everything has come together and it's worked out beautifully. I have the best customers in the world! They are such wonderful, understanding, life giving people. They definitely float my boat. I have so much to be grateful for! I tease my family since Myles was born, they manage to get to Tall Pines a lot more! I love it! Grandma has been struggling with health problems lately. I hate that! Wilma and many others are praying for her. My people are like family to me. I never realized how much they would effect my life. So much I have learned. Like how to get rid of a stye, by putting a gold ring on it. It takes out the fever. Hey, it works. Here' s one that's crazy but works. Myles was born with a clogged tear duct. The eye Doctor wanted to do a little surgery to unclog it. I was struggling with doing it. Dr. Mac told me one time, there is no such thing as a little surgery Hannah. All surgery come with risks. My little brother's best friend died having knee surgery at sixteen. So I do have concerns. I am sharing this with my banker and also dear friend Patty. She says, "this is your lucky day! I know how to fix it Hannah. You're going to think I'm crazy." "I already know you're crazy Patty, so tell me." We laugh. "Do you have a cloth diaper?" "Yes." "Okay, put it on Myles tonight and in the morning, squeeze the urine in his eye and let it sit. He's not going to like it, but hold him down and do it. I promise it will cure it." "Ok I'll try it. He will hate this story when he is older!" "Yes, he will but I did it to my son twenty-five years ago and it cured it! I do believe in the old remedies!" "I do too!" "Let me know." "Oh I will. Ben is going to freak out on this one! It's better than surgery!" "I agree." Went home that night and we did it, and it worked! Poor Myles! He was not happy with his parents! Wish he could understand it was to help him! We tried to explain, but not so sure he got it! He is cured, no more clogged tear duct! The Doctor just shook his head when I told him, but said "well it's clear, so you got lucky!" "Well I'll take it!" I said. I call Patty and tell her what happened and I say, "I'm a believer Patty!" "I told you it would work!" "Yes you did! Thank you for sharing Dr. Patty!" "Anytime Hannah! I'm so glad Myles didn't have to have a surgery." "Me too! Enjoy your day Patty!" "You too Hannah! Bye!"

• • •

So I realize the beauty shop has healing powers for just about anything. Sue said to me one time, "Hannah, we may not all be famous but we are all powerful!" I get that now. We all have the power to fan the flame in one another. That is a beautiful gift God has given us! We can also put out the flame! I want to be the fan!

CHAPTER 20

All's I'm Saying

"All's I'm saying Hannah, is I'm proud of you girl!" "Thank you Wilma!" "Look at you! I remember a little girl that was not sure who she was, and now I see a strong woman who is sure of who she is. I know you have made God smile!" "I hope so!"

• • •

I am looking in the mirror, seeing many people in me, and I have a vision of a crazy quilt. You know the ones that have all kinds of different patches and no certain pattern? I hear the voice of truth say, *Hannah that's how my children look.* You have patches from all the people you have touched, and have touched you. Some are little patches, some are larger one. All have been part of my perfect plan! Your reflection is of the many you have served and loved. Some of those patches hurt, but gave you more compassion and opened your heart to be a receiver, and a giver. Tears roll down my face as I see all the faces of the beauty shop, and I thank God that I'm a cosmetologist and not a marine biologist! I love my beauty shop life! I can't wait to see how the beauty shop evolves and for more conversations!

• • •

I would rather try and fail then never try at all.
You see, I've learned the pain of regret is much greater than
the pain of failure.
Dana

About the *Author*

Dana Williams was born in Las Cruces, N.M. She now lives in Ruidoso, N.M. with her husband Mark, of 31 years. She owns Bare Essentials Day Spa. They have two sons, Marcus and Samuel. Their family spends three months every summer in Naknek, Alaska, where they work side by side, commercial fishing for Wild Alaskan Salmon. They also run Willbros Salmon Company, and Naknek Who's There B&B. Dana also has Wild Alaska Tour Company. She loves Alaska and is passionate to share it's beauty with all.

Dana has always loved to journal and express her thoughts in writing. She has been a hair stylist (or hairdresser back in the day!) for 36 years. Twenty years ago the seed for this book was planted in her. She ignored it for many years, but continued to journal about life and the beauty shop. Although this book is fiction and no character is any true person, you may find bits and pieces of yourself in the different characters.

Dana is working on her next book. She continues to work at using up all God has put in her to create. She wants to inspire each and every person to live authentic lives, to not give up on their dreams, but to believe and live their dreams.

To learn more about the book and
Dana Williams, please visit
conversationsinthebeautyshop.com

Made in the USA
San Bernardino, CA
26 September 2017